Anonymous

Memorial Volume Of The Centenary Of St. Mary's Seminary Of St. Sulpice, Baltimore, Maryland, 1791-1891

Anonymous

Memorial Volume Of The Centenary Of St. Mary's Seminary Of St. Sulpice, Baltimore, Maryland, 1791-1891

ISBN/EAN: 9783744653398

Printed in Europe, USA, Canada, Australia, Japan

Cover: Foto ©ninafisch / pixelio.de

More available books at **www.hansebooks.com**

1791-1891

MEMORIAL VOLUME

OF THE

CENTENARY

—OF—

St. Mary's Seminary of St. Sulpice,

BALTIMORE, MD.

BALTIMORE:
JOHN MURPHY & CO.
1891.

TO

The Alumni

LIVING AND DEPARTED

OF

ST. MARY'S COLLEGE AND SEMINARY,

THIS

MEMORIAL VOLUME

IS

AFFECTIONATELY INSCRIBED.

CONTENTS.

	PAGE.
Historical Sketch of St. Mary's Seminary,	1
Superiors of St. Mary's Seminary,	37
Presidents of St. Mary's College,	38
Professors of St. Mary's Seminary,	39
Teachers, Tutors and other Officers of St. Mary's College,	41
Sulpicians at St. Charles' College, Mt. St. Mary's, and in the Missions,	47
Students of St. Mary's Seminary that have been ordained Priests,	49
Students of St. Mary's College,	79
Faculty of St. Mary's Seminary, 1891-92,	159
Faculty of St. Charles' College, 1891-92,	160
Students of St. Mary's Seminary, 1891-92,	161

LIST OF ILLUSTRATIONS.

	PAGE.
St. Mary's Seminary of St. Sulpice,	Frontispiece.
Jean Jacques Olier, Founder of the Seminary and of the Society of St. Sulpice,	1
Very Rev. Jacques André Emery, Ninth Superior-General of St. Sulpice,	4
Most Rev. John Carroll, D. D., First Archbishop of Baltimore,	8
The Old House which became the First Catholic Seminary in the United States,	12
Very Rev. François Charles Nagot, Founder and First Superior of St. Mary's Seminary,	16
Rt. Rev. John Dubois, Third Bishop of New York,	20
St. Mary's: College and Seminary,	24
St. Charles' College, Ellicott City, Md.,	28
Rt. Rev. B. J. Flaget, Bishop of Bardstown,	32
St. Mary's Seminary Chapel, Dedicated 1808,	36
Most Rev. Ambrose Maréchal, Third Archbishop of Baltimore,	42
Rev. O. L. Jenkins, First President of St. Charles' College,	46
Very Rev. Marie Jean Tessier, Second Superior of the Seminary,	49
Rev. Stephen T. Badin, the first Priest ordained in the United States, May 25, 1793,	50
Rev. Demetrius A. Galitzin,	50
Very Rev. Louis Régis Deluol, Third Superior of the Seminary,	54
Very Rev. François Lhomme, Fourth Superior of the Seminary,	58
Very Rev. Joseph Paul Dubreul, Fifth Superior of the Seminary,	64

	PAGE.
His Eminence James Cardinal Gibbons, Archbishop of Baltimore,	70
Very Rev. Alphonse Magnien, D. D., Superior of the Seminary,	76
Most Rev. William Dubourg, Founder and first President of St. Mary's College,	80
Rt. Rev. Simon G. Bruté, First Bishop of Vincennes,	93
Most Rev. Samuel Eccleston, D. D., Fifth Archbishop of Baltimore,	113
Rt. Rev. John J. Chanche, D. D., First Bishop of Natchez,	126
Rt. Rev. Augustin Verot, D. D., First Bishop of St. Augustine, Florida,	142
Faculty of St. Mary's Seminary, 1891–92,	159
Faculty of St. Charles' College, 1891–92,	160

JEAN JACQUES OLIER,
Founder of the Seminary and of the Society of St. Sulpice.

SEMINARY OF SAINT SULPICE,

BALTIMORE, MD.

1791-1891.

THE Seminary of St. Sulpice, Baltimore, generally known as St. Mary's Seminary, is a branch of the Seminary of St. Sulpice in Paris. Catholic seminaries owe their first origin to the Council of Trent. Cardinal Pallavicini, the historian of that council, speaking of measures taken for the reformation of the clergy, says: "The most important measure was, undoubtedly, the establishment of Seminaries. The Fathers hesitated not to declare that if the council should have no other result, the institution of Seminaries alone would more than compensate for all their labors; alone, it could restore neglected discipline, since in all commonwealths the people are what education makes them."[1] Among those raised by God to carry out the design of the Council in this particular, Jean Jacques Olier must hold an eminent rank. It was his special vocation to establish a Society whose

---

[1] *History of the Council of Trent*, Migne édit., 1845, Book xxi, Chap. viii.

object would be the training of young men for the priesthood. As the founder was also the pastor of the parish of St. Sulpice, Paris, the name of St. Sulpice clung to his Society. The Seminary, established by Father Olier in 1642, was the parent and model of many others throughout France, so that it may be truly said that the Society of St. Sulpice has been chiefly instrumental in forming the French clergy during the last 250 years.[1] The Revolution, which caused such ruin in the church of France, wrought untold blessings for other countries through the emigration of the clergy. The United States received a good share of that apostolate of the faithful priests who preferred exile and poverty to apostacy in their native land. When the cloud of religious persecution broke with unrestrained fury in Paris and the provinces, the Superior General of St. Sulpice was Jacques André Emery, a man whose broad views, extraordinary love of the Church, and invincible courage in face of the guillotine,[2] made his influence felt not only by the clergy of France, but even, later on, by the imperial potentate who wanted to subject the Church to his

---

[1] At the same time as he founded the Society of St. Sulpice, Father Olier organized with Mr. de la Dauversière an association for the colonizing of the island of Ville-Marie, or Montreal, Canada, and with his dying breath, in 1657, he gave orders that some members of his Society should be sent to that distant land to lay Christian faith and piety at the basis of the new colony. Hence the Sulpicians of Montreal have always been engaged in the external ministry, even since a College, and afterwards a Seminary of philosophy and theology, founded by them, have attained a high degree of prosperity.

[2] He was twice imprisoned for the faith, in 1793 and 1794, for sixteen months in daily expectation of the scaffold.

will. In 1790, Father Emery, in order, as he thought, to save his Society from destruction, had conceived the project of founding a colony of Sulpicians in the valley of the Mississippi, when he was informed that an episcopal See, the first in the United States, had just been erected in Baltimore. At the same time the papal nuncio, Mgr. Dugnani exhorted him to change his plan, and establish a Seminary in Maryland. Accordingly, Father Emery sent to England one of his priests, Father Nagot, to lay the design before Dr. Carroll, who had just been consecrated Bishop of Baltimore. At the first intimation of the project, the zealous pastor thanked God for this favorable opportunity of gratifying his own wishes and those of the Holy See by the establishment of a seminary in his diocese, but he declared that, as he had nothing to offer but his own good will, the Sulpicians would have to defray all expenses of traveling and installation. On Father Nagot's return to Paris, Providence supplied Father Emery with unexpected resources which enabled him to conclude at once the affair with the American prelate. The four Sulpicians selected for this important and distant mission were well qualified by their virtue, ability, and experience. Father François Charles Nagot, the first superior of the new Seminary, was 57 years of age when he came to America. He had filled with success some of the most important positions in the Society, and was considered one of its most learned and pious members. He had been successively professor of theology, president of the Preparatory Seminary, and vice-superior of the

Theological Seminary, in Paris. Among those who had selected him as their spiritual guide, it may be interesting to mention that celebrated Irish priest, the Abbé Edgeworth, who attended Louis XVI at the scaffold.[1] The three associates of Father Nagot were Fathers Garnier, Levadoux, and Tessier. Father Antoine Garnier was then 29 years old. He had taught divinity with great success in the Seminary of Lyons, and was a remarkable linguist. Father Michel Levadoux had been for many years a director of the Seminary of Bourges. Father Jean Tessier, born in 1758 in the diocese of Angers, had taught theology for two years at Viviers, when, in 1791, he was invited by Father Emery to join this little band. In order that the projected Seminary might be opened immediately, five Seminarians accompanied the pioneer Sulpicians. The travelers having chartered an American vessel, sailed from St. Malo in the month of March, and reached Baltimore July 10th, 1791. On the same ship there was a young Frenchman, then misled by Voltairian infidelity, but who, later on, consecrating his brilliant imagination and fascinating style to the service of religion, rendered illustrious the name of Chateaubriand.

Father Nagot, with his companions, after lodging for eight days at No. 94,[2] Market Street, rented for five hundred dollars a year a house then known as "The

[1] Madame Louise, sister of Louis XVI, on different occasions, sought the counsels of Father Nagot. He was also the means of converting several English protestants.
[2] The house has long since disappeared.

VERY REV. JACQUES ANDRÉ EMERY,
Ninth Superior General of St. Sulpice.

One Mile Tavern." This house, with four adjoining acres of land, was bought in September of the same year for $2,266.66, and there, October 3, 1791, the Sulpicians of Baltimore formally opened St. Mary's Seminary in the same spot that is now occupied by their successors in the centre of the city. The spiritual retreat was begun December 10th, and on the 15th of the same month, their first chapel having been dedicated, became the permanent abode of the Blessed Sacrament. In the following year, there were two other arrivals of Sulpicians—March 29th, Fathers Chicoisneau,[1] David,[2] and Flaget, with two students, Badin and Barret; June 24th, Fathers Maréchal, Richard, and Ciquard. Father Dubourg came to Baltimore in December, 1794,[3] and was admitted into the Society of St. Sulpice in 1795. All these priests, men of proved ability and virtue, were intended to work in the Seminary; but the want of pupils proved a bar to their activity and zeal. There were only five semi-

[1] Father Jean Baptiste Chicoisneau, a native of Orleans, had been for many years President of the Preparatory Seminary in the same city, when he was sent to Baltimore. Here he filled the position of Procurator in St. Mary's till 1796, when, at his request, he was transferred to the Sulpicians of Montreal. There he was made President of the College. He died in 1818.

[2] Father Jean Baptiste David, born in the diocese of Nantes, in 1761, was director of the Seminary of Angers, when that Seminary was closed by order of the National Assembly. Having come to Baltimore, he governed a little congregation at Secaia during eleven years, taught philosophy at Georgetown in 1803, and came back to St. Mary's in 1804.

[3] Rev. Louis Valentin du Bourg, or Dubourg, born in 1766 in the diocese of Bordeaux, was President of a Preparatory Seminary in Paris when the Revolution broke out. Obliged, in order to save his life, to disguise himself and emigrate to Spain, he finally resolved to come to the United States.

narians during the first three years, two in 1794, and none from 1795 to 1797; the number rose to twelve in 1804, but fell to eleven in 1806. The first priest ordained in the diocese of Baltimore was Rev. Theodore Badin. He had already studied theology at Orleans, in France, before he came to America. His ordination took place May 25th, 1793. Sent to Kentucky, he exercised the holy ministry with great zeal and success till his death in 1853. Of the two seminarians who were in St. Mary's in 1794, one was Prince Demetrius Galitzin. He belonged to the highest nobility of Russia. His father, being ambassador at the Hague, sent the young prince under the pseudonym of Smith to travel in America. The acquaintance made in Baltimore with the gentlemen of the Seminary, led to his conversion. He entered the Seminary in 1792, was ordained in 1795, and joined the Society of St. Sulpice. He did not, however, remain in the Seminary, having promised Bishop Carroll to work in the missions. After exercising his apostolate in Virginia and Maryland, he finally fixed his residence at Loretto, Cambria County, Pennsylvania. There he died, in 1846, with the reputation of great sanctity, having brought into the fold of the Catholic Church more than six thousand Protestants. The first American seminarian was William Matthews, nephew of Archbishop Neale, who, ordained in 1800, was for nearly fifty years the worthy pastor of St. Patrick's Church, Washington. We shall not be surprised at the scarcity of seminarians, if we reflect that the Catholics, at that epoch, were few and far scattered, and that Georgetown was for some time the only Catholic College in the country. The few young men who entered the ecclesiastical state were generally employed as teachers or prefects at their Alma Mater. The directors themselves of the Seminary were at times requested by Bishop Carroll to lend their services to that institution. Thus Father Flaget taught at Georgetown from 1795 to 1798, Father Dubourg was President of the same establishment from September, 1796, to January 7th, 1799, and Father Maréchal was professor of philosophy there in 1801. Several Sulpicians, according to the desire of Father Emery, even devoted either a few years, or their whole life, to the work of the missions. Father Ciquard, after announcing the good tidings of the Gospel to the Indians of Passamaquoddy, Maine, ended his career in Montreal in 1824. Fathers Levadoux, Flaget, and Dilhet, labored for a time among the Illinois. Father Gabriel Richard, the apostle of Michigan, wrought with undiminished zeal till 1832, when he died a victim of cholera.[1] Nearer home in Maryland, Fathers Garnier, Maréchal, Tessier, and David, exercised the ministry at the Point[2] in Baltimore, at Winchester, Carroll Manor, and elsewhere.[3]

[1] A statue has been erected to his memory in Detroit, the central field of his labors. Imprisoned on account of the debts contracted in building St. Ann's Church, Detroit, he had himself elected to Congress in order to recover his liberty, and gain the means to pay his debts. He is the only priest that ever sat in Congress.

[2] For many years St. Patrick's Church was called the Church of the Point, and the place was Fell's Point.

[3] Father Garnier was the first pastor of St. Patrick's congregation, Baltimore, and it was under his direction that the corner-stone of the first church was laid.

The urgent necessity of procuring clerics for the Seminary, suggested the idea of opening a school or academy. Even as early as 1793, the Sulpicians of St. Mary's gathered together a few children to whom they taught the rudiments of French and Latin. This first effort, however, was discontinued after a year, because it was feared that this school would keep students from Georgetown College. But on the 20th of August, 1799, Father Dubourg, having brought three young Spaniards from Havana, opened with these and a few French boys what was called St. Mary's Academy. The students were lodged in the Seminary till the following year, when a new building was erected, and the name of Academy was changed into that of College. But the Spanish government, taking some umbrage at the emigration of the young Cubans to Baltimore, ordered them all back. The measure was executed September 20th, 1803. Before this time the number of students allowed in the Academy by Bishop Carroll had been limited first to twelve, then extended to twenty-five. No American boy had been admitted into St. Mary's College through deference for the bishop and the administrators of Georgetown, but now it became a necessity to do otherwise. In the Fall of 1803, it was announced that the doors of St. Mary's College would be open to all American students, day-scholars or boarders, without distinction of creed. Many boys at once flocked to the Institution. The brilliancy of the Literary Entertainments and the solemn distribution of rewards before a large concourse

Most Rev. John Carroll, D. D.,
First Archbishop of Baltimore.

of people, at the Annual Commencement, attracted attention and spread the reputation of the College all over the States and even abroad. In January, 1805, the Legislature of Maryland raised St. Mary's to the rank of a University, empowering it to *admit any of its students to any degree or degrees in any of the faculties, arts, and sciences, and liberal professions, which are usually permitted to be conferred in any Colleges or Universities in America or Europe.* It was at the Commencement of 1806, August 13th, that the academical degrees were conferred for the first time.[1] The number of pupils in that year amounted to one hundred and six. Additional buildings had then been erected, and others were in progress. The great hall used for public occasions, was large enough to accommodate one thousand attendants. The chapel, the corner-stone of which was laid June 18th, 1806, and the dedication made in 1808, was for many years considered the most beautiful in the United States. Under the management of Mr. La Thulaye, there arose within the enclosure of the College, a superb botanical garden with a large collection of domestic and foreign plants. When, in 1816, Mr. La Thulaye took away his botanical garden, it was replaced by another of still greater proportions, which remained till the suppression of the College in 1852. The grounds, forming an area of about seven acres, were tastefully

---

[1] The successful candidates were Jules De Menon, J. B. Maurau, Nicholas A. de Mun, and Theodore Trigant. On this occasion, the degrees of A. B. and A. M. were also bestowed on Robert Walsh, who had been a student in 1800 and 1801.

laid out with a view to the health and recreation of the students. The rapid development of St. Mary's College, within a few years of its foundation, was due to the exceptional merit of its professors, and especially of its first president, Rev. William Dubourg, a man of eminent talents, brilliant eloquence, and great experience in the art of training youth. But, whilst he raised the College to such a height of prosperity, his management of temporal matters was too liberal, and he thereby involved himself and his confrères in considerable difficulties. In return for the privilege of a lottery which he obtained from the Legislature, he contracted the obligation of maintaining St. Mary's College for thirty years or forfeiting $30,000. At the end of his administration, the House was so in debt that it took many years of the strictest economy to retrieve its finances. He remained at his post till the year 1812, when he was called to New Orleans to be administrator, and, later on, bishop of that diocese.[1] Father Dubourg, in his presidency of St. Mary's College, was ably seconded by his associates. Among these we may mention particularly the Sulpicians Flaget and David, besides the Rev. M. Paquict, and Mr. de Chevigné. Father Flaget, by the earnestness of his religious instructions and the eminence of his virtue, exerted a lasting and most

---

[1] He resigned his See of New Orleans in 1824, was transferred to that of Montauban, and, in 1833, became Archbishop of Besançon, where he died the same year. We may add that the name of Bishop Dubourg is intimately connected with the origin of the Propagation of the Faith. It was in response to his appeal in behalf of his diocese that the first contributions were raised, and the first organization of that admirable work was started.

beneficial influence on the character of the students. Designated by Bishop Carroll, and appointed by Pope Pius VII, in 1809, to create and govern the diocese of Bardstown, Kentucky, he was overwhelmed at the news, and had no peace until Father Emery ordered him to submit, allowing him at the same time to remain a Sulpician. It is not the place here to dwell on his virtues of humility and simplicity, his hardships and labors, nor even on the abundant fruits of sanctity, which distinguished the forty years of his episcopal administration. By the side of Father Flaget in St. Mary's, was the learned and sagacious Father David, who taught philosophy with great success from 1805 to 1811, and whose conferences, every Wednesday evening, drew considerable attention. He followed his venerable friend to Bardstown, and was compelled to share with him the burden of the episcopate. The Rev. Mr. Paquiet was a French priest of superior ability, who taught eloquence and natural philosophy from 1802 to 1812. He had the principal hand in the direction of the College under Father Dubourg, and was his successor in the office of president. Among the lay professors, the most distinguished was Mr. de Chevigné, an old sea-captain, well versed in mathematics, who devoted to teaching the last twenty-four years of his life (1802–1826).

The remarkable prosperity of the College did not, however, fully subserve the end for which the Seminary of Baltimore had been founded, that is, the formation of a native clergy. From the beginning, Father Emery had insisted upon the establishment of clerical schools, which would be a nursery for the Seminary. Thus he wrote to Father Nagot in 1792: "If American priests be not prepared in numbers sufficient for the needs of the American church, nothing, or only present good, will be achieved. Foreigners can never be in sufficient numbers, nor as fit as native priests. Numerous schools should be established, in order that proper subjects may be found for philosophy and theology." The Academy or College, founded at Georgetown in 1789, far from supplying subjects, on the contrary took from the Seminary the clerics that were most fit for teaching. In order to comply with the views of Father Emery and the wishes of Father Nagot, an attempt had been made at founding a clerical school in 1793, but it proved to be abortive. Six years later, when St. Mary's Academy was opened, it too was very nearly stifled in its birth, as we may judge from the following letter of Father Emery to Bishop Carroll: "I had advised the gentlemen of the Seminary, according to the council of Trent, to educate young men showing some disposition for the priesthood; but Father Nagot has informed me that you did not assent to this measure for fear of harming Georgetown College. I respect your intentions and honor your wisdom, and at the distance I am from Baltimore, it is not proper for me to judge of the reasons of your opposition. But it seems to me that the consideration of forming priests for the United States is of paramount importance; for what would be a diocese with none but foreign priests, who are often unknown, and dependent upon temporary

The Old House which became the First Catholic Seminary in the U. S.

circumstances? Father Nagot informs me that, to avoid this inconvenient state of things, some young men are now brought up by the gentlemen of the Seminary; but his letters show that you are somewhat displeased at this measure. I have the honor of declaring to you, *Monseigneur*, that I shall never approve any measure of the gentlemen of the Seminary which would meet an earnest and continued opposition on your part. Such an approbation would be contrary to the spirit of my Society, which must depend on bishops. Consequently, I have not approved the establishment of the Academy, since it had not your approbation."[1] Bishop Carroll, on the strength of this letter, resolved on suppressing the Academy within two or three years. Meantime Father Emery, seeing on the one hand an opportunity of reëstablishing seminaries in France and the urgent need of all his priests for that object, and noticing, on the other hand, the little result of the Seminary of Baltimore after a great expenditure of men and money, resolved on gradually recalling all the Sulpicians from the United States. Being informed of this design, Bishop Carroll was alarmed, and wrote several urgent letters to Father Emery to deter him from his resolution. "I declare to you," he said, "as I have declared it in every circumstance, that I have nowhere else known men more able than your priests, by their character, talents, and virtues, to form such clergymen as the state of religion demands

---

[1] Letter of Father Emery to Bishop Carroll, August 9th, 1800.

now. Accordingly, I believe that it would be one of the greatest misfortunes that could befall this diocese ever to lose the gentlemen of the Seminary. This sentiment is so deeply impressed upon my mind that I was overwhelmed when I heard that you had thought for a moment of recalling them. I earnestly beseech you to banish this idea from your mind, and to be assured that they will actually fulfil the views of your Company and the end for which you have sent them here."[1] "I beseech you, by the merciful heart of Jesus, not to take them all away, and, if it be necessary for me to bear the terrible trial of seeing the greater number of them depart, I implore you at least to leave here a germ which may produce fruit in the season decreed by the Lord."[2] Several other letters passed on this subject between Bishop Carroll and the Superior of St. Sulpice. All the Sulpicians in the United States, although they felt an extreme repugnance to leave America, were ready to comply with the desire of their Superior General. The bishop insisted particularly on retaining Fathers Garnier and Maréchal, for whom he felt unbounded esteem and affection. "You are not obliged to leave," said he to Father Garnier, "Father Emery does not command you by virtue of holy obedience." "*Monseigneur*," replied Father Garnier, "we Sulpicians take no vows, and our superiors generally do not use words of command. It is enough for me to know the will of my superior. As I know

[1] January, 1801.   [2] September, 1801.

it surely, I could not otherwise have the certainty of doing the will of God, I would enjoy no peace, and so, in spite of my repugnance to depart from you, *Monseigneur*, and return to France, I am determined to leave at once." "The good bishop," said Father Garnier, "shed tears, and on the day of my departure, he refused to see anybody, and did not leave his room even to take his meal." Fathers Garnier,[1] Levadoux, and Cathelin actually left Baltimore, May 23d, 1803, and Father Maréchal, July 4th. The return of Father Nagot to Paris was considered so certain that the Assembly of St. Sulpice, held in October, 1802, appointed him one of the four Consultors. He would actually have departed in 1804, if the state of his health had allowed, but an attack of apoplexy, experienced in 1795, had left him ever after in a precarious condition. Meantime, a change was wrought in the mind of Father Emery. When, in 1804, Pius VII went to Paris for the coronation of Napoleon, Father Emery laid before the Holy Father the project he had formed of recalling all his subjects from Baltimore: "My son," answered the venerable pontiff, "let it stand —yes, let that Seminary stand; for it will bear fruit in its own time. To recall its directors in order to employ them here in other seminaries, would be to rob Peter to pay Paul." Father Emery received these words as an

---

[1] Father Garnier taught the Scriptures and the Oriental languages in the Seminary of Paris with the highest distinction. His eminent talents, his prudence, and his perfect obedience, gained the love and confidence of Father Emery. He was Superior General of the Company from 1826 to 1845.

oracle from heaven. He never more contemplated the design of abandoning Baltimore, and Providence took upon itself in its own good time to justify the decision of the Holy Father.

The measure, taken 1803, of receiving subjects without discrimination of creed or aspiration, while it gave impetus to St. Mary's College, destroyed its peculiar character of Preparatory Seminary. It became a mixed College, and comparatively few subjects found or preserved there a clerical vocation. The saintly superior of the Seminary, Father Nagot, preoccupied, as Father Emery himself was, with the idea of having purely ecclesiastical schools, began, in 1806, a new establishment at Pigeon-hill, Adams County, Pennsylvania. A suitable tract of land had been given for that object by Mr. Joseph Harent, a French Catholic, who, later on, was ordained, and joined the Society of St. Sulpice. Here Father Nagot gathered a dozen promising children of the neighborhood, who all desired to become priests, and with the aid of a few seminarians, trained them to literature and piety. It was a touching spectacle to see that venerable priest, who, for many years, had reckoned among his pupils or penitents the élite of the French capital, consuming the last remains of his strength in teaching the rudiments of the Latin language to a few children of humble condition, and considering this occupation as the glory and comfort of his old age.

When, two years afterwards, the College of Pigeon-hill was transferred to Emmitsburg, Father Nagot came back to St. Mary's, sharing with his confrères the work

VERY REV. FRANCOIS CHARLES NAGOT,
Founder and First Superior of St. Mary's Seminary.

of the ministry not only in behalf of the French, then numerous in Baltimore, but also of the English-speaking population, in spite of his difficulty in pronouncing their language. On account of his infirmities and love of retirement, he had oftentimes offered the resignation of his office of superior, but it was not accepted till the year 1810, which was also the fiftieth of his priesthood. He spent the remainder of his life in the practice of obedience to the new superior, asking all permissions with the simplicity of a young cleric. He edified the whole community by the example of his faith, humility, devotion to the Blessed Sacrament, love of prayer, application to the reading of the Scriptures, and zeal for the salvation of souls and the sanctification of priests. Eminent by his virtues in his lifetime, he died with the reputation of great sanctity, March 9th, 1816.[1]

When Father Nagot resigned in 1810, the charge of Superior passed into the hands of Father Tessier, one of the four earliest Sulpicians sent to Baltimore in 1791. Outside of his occupations in St. Mary's Seminary as teacher or treasurer, he had been actively engaged in the ministry, giving his predilection to the colored people. Now his new office laid upon him the general care of the three Sulpician institutions, St. Mary's Seminary and College, and the College lately founded at Emmitsburg

---

[1] Father Nagot was the author or translator of several works, among which we may particularly mention his excellent *Vie de M. Olier*, composed at the request of Father Emery, but published only in 1818 by Father Duclaux, then Superior General of St. Sulpice.

by Father Dubois. This last zealous priest, who, at the beginning of the French revolution, was a curate of the parish of St. Sulpice, Paris, had come to the United States in 1791.[1] Appointed by Bishop Carroll to the numerous and extensive missions of which Fredericktown was the centre, Father Dubois had occasion to renew his acquaintance with St. Sulpice. Every year he would come to St. Mary's Seminary for his spiritual retreat, and finally, December 6th, 1808, he sought and obtained admission into their society, without discontinuing his work in the missions. But a new field was offered to his zeal, when Father Dubourg suggested to him the idea of founding a Preparatory Seminary at the Mountain near Emmitsburg. Entering upon this design, Father Dubois transferred to the Sulpicians, with the consent of Bishop Carroll, a small property which he owned there, together with his house and church. Other adjacent lands, amounting to five hundred acres, were bought by Fathers Dubourg and Dubois in the name of the Society, new buildings were erected, and, even before their completion, in the spring of 1809, the sixteen students of Pigeon-hill[2] joined the young men already gathered by Father Dubois. The school took the name of Mount St. Mary's College. The number of pupils having risen to sixty in 1811, and the only

[1] The letters of recommendation which he brought with him, especially some from Lafayette, gave him an easy access to several eminent Americans, particularly President Monroe and Patrick Henry. The latter had the patience and kindness of acting as English teacher to the missioner.

[2] The property of Pigeon-hill remained in the possession of the Seminary, serving as a residence during vacation, till the year 1849.

help available being one seminarian, John Hickey, it became a necessity for Father Dubois to employ the most advanced students in teaching the others. As if the pastoral care of Father Dubois, extending over several counties, and the charge of the College, were not enough for his devouring activity, he was also appointed Superior to the community of Sisters of St. Joseph, just founded at Emmitsburg by Mother Seton. Most timely and useful was the assistance granted him in 1812 by the arrival of another active laborer in the Lord's vineyard, Father Bruté, who, like Father Dubois, has left his impress on the College of the Mountain. Father Simon Guillaume Gabriel Bruté de Rémur, of a respectable family of Rennes, in little Brittany, had received with highest honors the degree of Doctor of Medicine in Paris, in 1803, being then twenty-four years of age. But entering that same year the Seminary of St. Sulpice, Paris, and being soon after admitted into the Society, he came to America (1810). From the moment of his appointment to Mount St. Mary's College he devoted his energies to the welfare of that Institution. There he remained, with the exception of three years (1815-1818), till he was consecrated the first bishop of Vincennes, in 1834. Among the troubles which weighed heavily upon the President of Mt. St. Mary's and his associate, the debts arising from first installation and the gratuitous support of indigent pupils, were not the least. These difficulties at last led Father Dubois to admit not only young men who had no inclination for the priesthood, but even non-Catholics, and thus the character of the College as a purely clerical school was changed. As Father Tessier, who was responsible as Superior of the Sulpicians in the United States, feared that the debts of the Mountain might involve the Seminary of Baltimore, and precipitate both into irretrievable ruin, he transferred to Father Dubois his legal title to the property of Emmitsburg, in order that the latter might hold it in the name of the Society, as he himself had held it (1819). Later on, in 1826, the Superior General of St. Sulpice abandoned the whole actual property at Emmitsburg to Father Dubois, with the sole condition that the latter would assume the responsibility of the debts. Thus was cut off the dependence of Mt. St. Mary's College on the Society, and, as a consequence, Fathers Dubois, Bruté, and Xaupi, ceased to belong to St. Sulpice; but the closest bonds of friendship and intercourse continued to exist. When, in the same year, 1826, Father Dubois was appointed to the see of New York, it was in St. Mary's Seminary, Baltimore, that he made his spiritual retreat, preparatory to his consecration. It were hard to exaggerate the beneficent influence of the well-known Institution founded by Fathers Dubois and Bruté. It has justly been called 'the mother of bishops;' it has given to America its first Cardinal, and trained for the State many able and distinguished citizens.

RT. REV. JOHN DU BOIS, D. D.,
Third Bishop of New York.

The administration of Father Tessier as Superior of St. Mary's Seminary lasted from 1810 to 1829. His constant and unostentatious efforts were seconded by several other Sulpicians of great worth. Prominent among these was Father Ambrose Maréchal, who, after an absence of nine years in France (1803–1812), had returned to the field of his former labors. His learning, eloquence, piety, sweet and firm disposition, made him the most trusted support of the Seminary. After having refused the sees of New York and Philadelphia, at the instance of the Superior of St. Sulpice, he accepted that of Baltimore under the assurance of remaining in the Society. His Bulls of coadjutor of Archbishop Neale having arrived after the death of the latter, he was at once acknowledged Archbishop of Baltimore, and consecrated, December 14th, 1817. He had brought with him from France, in 1812, a young deacon, Rev. Edward Damphoux, who soon after was admitted into the Company of St. Sulpice, and was for nine years President of the College. Mr. Joseph Harent, the donor of Friendly Hall or Pigeon-hill, rendered eminent services by his judicious administration of the finances.[1] Two other Sulpicians, Fathers Coupé and Tiphaigne, destined for Baltimore, after having been twice captured by the English, perished at sea, and with them were lost a number of books, and several precious vestments that had belonged to Father Olier. The arrival of Fathers Louis Deluol and J. B. Randanne, in 1817, served to

---

[1] Having gone to the Antilles to collect sums of money due to the College, he died in Martinique, April 10th, 1818.

fill up the vacancies made by the promotion of Father Maréchal and the premature death of Father Harent. Later on, Fathers J. H. Joubert,[1] John Hickey,[2] Alexius Elder,[3] Michael Wheeler,[4] John Larkin,[5] and J. J. Chanche, came to enlarge the little band of Seminary priests, who worked with so much zeal and ability under the direction of Father Tessier. Models themselves of every Christian and sacerdotal virtue, they left an indelible impression on the character of the youths whom they trained. Among these we may name Andrew

[1] Father Joubert was the founder of the colored sisterhood of Oblates, who continue to this day to instruct young negro girls. His zeal for the colored people is more worthy of notice, when we know what his relatives and himself had suffered from that race. Born in France, in 1777, he had come in 1800 to San Domingo, and was compelled to leave in 1803. Ordained in Baltimore, in 1810, and placed at the College, he gained the reputation of being an accomplished disciplinarian.

[2] John Francis Hickey, born in Maryland, in 1789, studied at St. Mary's College, and was ordained in 1814. He was variously occupied at Emmitsburg, St. Mary's Seminary, and in the parochial ministry till his death in 1869. He was remarkable through life for the simplicity and straightforwardness of his manners, and his absolute docility to the will of his superiors.

[3] Alexius Joseph Elder, born at Emmitsburg, in 1791, and received into the Society in 1822, rendered great services as prefect, and keeper of the books. Both he and Father Hickey lived to celebrate the golden jubilee of their priesthood. He died in 1871.

[4] Michael Francis Wheeler, born in Harford, Maryland, in 1796, was ordained in 1820. Gifted with splendid talents, but infirm in health, he taught various branches, was President of the College for a few months in 1827, and died prematurely in 1832.

[5] John Larkin, born in New Castle, England, February 2nd, 1801, came to Baltimore, September 9th, 1825, and was ordained in 1827. Soon after, the Sulpicians of Montreal having asked for help, Father Larkin was sent to them. He joined the Jesuits in 1840, and died in New York in 1858. A man of remarkable attainments, he was particularly distinguished for his knowledge of Greek.

Bienvenue Roman,[1] J. H. B. Latrobe,[2] Samuel Eccleston,[3] George A. Carrell,[4] J. A. Reynolds,[5] Thomas Heyden, Edward Knight, Charles I. White, John Hoskyns, and many others. Pope Pius VII wishing to acknowledge the services rendered by St. Mary's Seminary and College, and encourage new efforts in the future, was pleased by Letters dated April 18, 1822, to endow the institution with all the privileges of Catholic Universities. The first to receive the doctorate of divinity were Fathers Whitfield, vicar-general of the diocese of Baltimore, Deluol, and Damphoux. The degree was conferred with great solemnity in the Baltimore Cathedral, by Archbishop Maréchal acting in the name of the Pope (January 25, 1824). Five years later, Father Tessier resigned the burden of his office in the hands of Father Carrière, official visitor for the Superior-General of St. Sulpice; and henceforth lived in retirement till his death in 1840.

The new superior was Father Louis Deluol, who had already lived twelve years in Baltimore, had been President of the College for one year, and for three years Superior General of the Sisters of St. Joseph, Emmitsburg. He resigned this last busy office, when he was made President of the Seminary, but the resignation did not take off from him the principal part in the direction

---

[1] Twice Governor of Louisiana, and a distinguished statesman. Born in Opelousas, La., March, 1785, he died in New Orleans, January, 1866.

[2] The celebrated lawyer, engineer, and man of letters, whose death has just occurred.

[3] The fifth Archbishop of Baltimore.

[4] The first bishop of Covington. [5] The second bishop of Charleston, S. C.

of the Institute. He was even obliged, in 1841, to assume the official title again, and keep it, in spite of all efforts to the contrary, till finally, through his instrumentality, the Sisters of St. Joseph of Mother Seton were united with the Sisters of Charity of St. Vincent de Paul.

Father Deluol's broadness of mind, the versatility of his talent, his business abilities, his activity, and the geniality of his manners—all combined, together with his official position, to make him one of the most influential and popular clergymen in America. "Having much to do in spiritual and temporal matters, he often encountered great difficulties, and rendered to the Seminary services which should never be forgotten. Obliged by the circumstances to exercise the ministry, he brought back to the Church a large number of heretics. He was called by the confidence of the Most Rev. Archbishops of Baltimore to share not only in the administration of the diocese, but also in all the most important measures then enacted in behalf of the American Church. He took an active part in the seven provincial Councils held in Baltimore from 1829 to 1849."[1]

Under Father Deluol's stimulating influence, the College, which for a few years had lost ground, reached its highest degree of prosperity. The Baltimore *American* was able to say, in 1830: "We believe that no institution of the kind possesses a body of officers and tutors more able and zealous in the execution of the tasks which they have undertaken." We have

[1] Circular Letter of Father Carrière, Superior General of St. Sulpice, December 10, 1858.

before us *The Calendar of St. Mary's College* for the academic year 1833-4, which we quote as the best encomium upon that Institution :

FACULTY, TUTORS, AND OTHER OFFICERS:

REV. S. ECCLESTON, A. M., *President,*
REV. JOHN J. CHANCHE, *Vice-President.*

REV. L. DELUOL, S. T. D.,	MICHAEL P. GALLIGHER,
REV. AUGUSTIN VÉROT,	HENRY B. COSKERY, A. B.,
REV. FRANCIS LHOMME,	HENRY H. BURGESS,
REV. JAMES H. JOUBERT,	JOHN P. DONELAN,
J. A. PIZARRO, A. M.,	EDWARD J. CHAISTY, A. B.,
REV. JOHN B. RANDANNE,	MICHAEL WALSH,
REV. ALEXIUS J. ELDER,	HUGH GRIFFIN,
REV. PETER FRÉDET,	JAMES STRAIN,
REV. EDWARD KNIGHT, A. M.,	HERVEY COLBURN,
REV. JOHN H. HOSKYNS, A. M.,	JOHN NENNINGER,
REV. HENRY MYERS, A. B.,	PATRICK KELLY,
REV. SYLVESTER B. PIOT,	SAMUEL SMITH.

The students of that year numbered one hundred and ninety-five. The largest number in the Calendars that we possess, is two hundred and seven for the academic year 1839-40. The President, Samuel Eccleston, a Marylander by birth, was a Protestant in religion, when, at the age of thirteen, he entered St. Mary's College. There he studied his classics with considerable success, became a Catholic and a priest. After two years spent in France, returning to this country as a Sulpician, he taught in St. Mary's

College, and was appointed its President in 1829, at the age of twenty-eight. The five years of his office were for the Institution an era of prosperity, during which science, discipline, and piety, flourished. Selected to be the coadjutor of Archbishop Whitfield, in 1834, he accepted the honorable burden by the advice of Father Garnier, the Superior of St. Sulpice, and remained a member of the Society. Having become, in the same year, Archbishop of Baltimore, he ruled the diocese with prudence and kindness for sixteen years, conciliating all by the dignity of his person and the suavity of his manners. He held five provincial Councils, over which he presided with singular ability and wisdom. His successor in the presidency of the College was Rev. J. J. Chanche, S. S., a Baltimorean, a type of the accomplished gentleman, and he, too, was called to wear a mitre as first Bishop of Natchez, in 1841. Among the distinguished members of the Faculty, several others demand also a special mention. Father Vérot, S. S., acquired a well-deserved reputation in the teaching of higher mathematics and natural philosophy, and was often consulted by members of learned societies. Appointed Vicar Apostolic of Florida, in 1858, he was also made Bishop of Savannah, Georgia, 1861, and transferred, 1870, to St. Augustine, Florida, where he died in 1876. Truly apostolic in his ways, a man of learning and of wit, he was humble and unassuming as a child. Father Lhomme was the chief professor of Greek in St. Mary's, Father Randanne, of Latin. Father Frédet, D. D., is well known for his excellent text-books on history, which, however, give but a faint idea of his deep learning in that and other branches. Father E. Knight was acknowledged a model of scholarly elegance in his native tongue. Father Hoskyns, prematurely carried off (1835) by a violent contagion, left behind him deep regrets that his varied accomplishments were nipped almost in the bud. If the teachers of St. Mary's, especially between 1830 and 1840, were men of superior ability, it were hard, on the other hand, to exaggerate the respect and admiration which the alumni have kept to this day for the men who had charge of them. These sentiments, honorable alike to professors and pupils, extend to the whole history of the College. Never were alumni more proud of their Alma Mater than the students of old St. Mary's.

Fathers G. N. Raymond and O. L. Jenkins were the last two Presidents. The former, a man of versatile talents, always ready for any emergency, fulfilled the office from 1841 to 1849; the name of the latter is inseparably connected with the history of another institution—St. Charles' College, the origin and development of which claim now our attention.

The Sulpicians had always entertained the desire of founding a Preparatory College, exclusively devoted to the formation and education of clerics. It was to gratify this desire and contribute his share to the development of the Church, that Charles Carroll of Carrollton had, in 1830, donated two hundred and fifty-three acres of land, contiguous to his domain, and obtained from the General Assembly of Maryland a

Charter of Incorporation, which vested the legal title of St. Charles' College in the hands of five trustees. The first of these, selected by Charles Carroll himself—Fathers Deluol, Chanche, Elder, Tessier, and Eccleston—were authorized to possess the given property and acquire additional revenues, on condition that these would be employed in educating young Catholics for the ministry of the Gospel. Soon after, the donor sent the following letter to Father Deluol:

BALTIMORE, 27 *March*, 1830.

My dear Sir:

Mr. Reed will deliver to you from me the Deed of St. Charles' Seminary, and a certificate for fifty shares of United States Bank stock, which gift I wish to remain under the charge of the Sulpicians—that the trustees may be chosen from their Society, and not from the general body of the clergy.

I request that Mass may be said once a month for myself and family.

I rely upon your promise that the land may remain in my possession as long as it is agreeable to me to retain it. That this gift may be useful to religion, and aid our Church in rearing those who will guide us in the way of truth, is the fervent prayer of

Your sincere friend,

CH. CARROLL OF CARROLLTON.

Rev^d *Mr. Deluol,*
    Sup^r *of the Sulpicians.*

By a vote of the trustees and in their name, Father Deluol answered as follows:

St. Mary's Sem^y, Balt., *March* 29th, 1830.

Respected and Dear Sir :

Mr. Reed delivered to me on Saturday afternoon the Deed of St. Charles' Seminary and a certificate for fifty shares of United States Bank stock, accompanied by your very obliging letter. Your wish respecting the occupancy of the land shall be religiously observed. Mass shall be said, at least, once a month, for yourself and family in St. Charles' chapel.

It would be presumptuous, my Dear Sir, to offer you *our* acknowledgments for a donation which gives you a claim to the gratitude of the whole American Church. Yet, as you have made us the channel of your pious and enlightened liberality, we may be allowed to say that we appreciate the honor implied in the choice. St. Charles' Seminary will not, we pledge ourselves, be unfaithful to the memory of its venerable and illustrious Founder. Impressed in its origin with the moral dignity associated with his name, it will be a lasting monument of his princely munificence.

That it may, Respected and Dear Sir, contribute to extend the benefits of religion, and be an earnest of every blessing for you and your family, is our sincere wish, and shall be our constant prayer.

With great respect

Your most obed^t & humble serv^t,

L. Deluol.

Hon. Ch. Carroll of Carrollton.

The corner-stone of the first building was blessed by Archbishop Whitfield, in 1831, in presence of the venerable patriot who was then in the ninety-fourth year of his age. But the funds at the disposal of the Trustees were not sufficient to push the construction rapidly.

In April, 1832, Father Deluol, writing to the Council for the Propagation of the Faith in order to enlist their interest in the new institution, says: "The Sulpicians of Baltimore have indeed in the city a College (St. Mary's), which has rendered and still renders great services to religion. Some Protestant boys have embraced the Catholic religion with the consent of their parents; others who continue in their religion, learn to know and esteem ours, and to be its defenders and apologists in the world. This College has also, every year, formed some subjects for the Church, and from it have come nearly all the priests that have been educated in the Seminary. Nevertheless, experience has proved that it does not fully attain the principal object for which it was founded, the preparing of candidates for the Church. To support this institution, it is necessary to admit children of every denomination, a circumstance which precludes from clerical students a training specially adapted to their vocation; and, besides, it is to be feared that some vocations are not developed for want of proper environments, and others are lost in the medley crowd of boys, who, being richly born, do not relish a life of sacrifice and self-denial, which, however, is essential to the priesthood." These views of Father Deluol are also expressed by Archbishop Eccleston, in a letter written, January 31st, 1838, to the same Association. The prelate then adds these details: "A few years ago, we began to build a house for a Preparatory Seminary, a few miles from Baltimore. We have done all that was in our power to complete this purely Ecclesiastical College, and put it in operation; but the lack of pecuniary resources has compelled us to suspend the work and wait, till Providence come to our aid." Owing therefore to financial difficulties, also to the want of ready subjects, and perhaps to a certain hesitation in face of a new, arduous, and uncertain enterprise, St. Charles' College was not opened before 1848. The merit of the initiative is principally due to the Most Rev. S. Eccleston, and Father O. L. Jenkins, who was appointed first President of the Institution by the Archbishop with the sanction of the Superior of St. Sulpice. Father Deluol, whose health, originally very robust, had been several times stricken, was recalled to Paris in 1849. "After two years devoted to the recruiting of his strength, he took his rank among the directors of the Paris Seminary, and was appointed professor of Hebrew. He always showed the most exemplary exactness in attending the exercises of the Community, and merited by the goodness of his heart the affection of his confrères and of all who dealt with him. Oftentimes we have witnessed bishops, missioners, and other persons of distinction, eager, on their arrival from America, to visit him, and give him evidence of their esteem, kindness, and confidence."[1] During Father Deluol's administration of St. Mary's Seminary, the most noted alumni were F. X. Leray (late Archbishop of New Orleans), John McGill (late Bishop of Richmond), D. W. Bacon (the first Bishop of Portland,

[1] Circular Letter of the Superior General, Father Carrière, December 10th, 1858.

Mc.), Thomas Foley (late Bishop of Chicago), E. P. Wadhams (the present Bishop of Ogdensburg), J. McCaffrey, E. McColgan (Mgr., V. G.), B. J. McManus (Mgr.), W. A. Blenkinsop, O. L. Jenkins, Henry Coskery, H. F. Griffin, J. J. Dougherty, F. E. Boyle, H. J. Parke, J. A. Walter.

Very Rev. François Lhomme succeeded Father Deluol (1849). It was the task of the new superior to reorganize St. Mary's Seminary by disentangling it from the College, in order that the clerics should give their whole time and application to the duties of their state of life. The Sulpicians had always claimed that their special vocation was to form young men for the priesthood, and not for secular professions. But till then difficulties, which they deemed insurmountable, had prevented them from carrying out their normal object. Now the circumstances which had led them to engage in the functions of the ministry and the work of the College had passed away, and four years of ever-growing prosperity had proved the success of the new Preparatory College of St. Charles. It was under the influence of these views that the Superior of St. Sulpice, Father de Courson, decided upon suppressing St. Mary's College, and stopping the exercise of the external ministry.[1] The College was actually closed in 1852, and, through an understanding with the Jesuit Fathers, the vacancy was filled at once by the founding of Loyola College. Thirty-nine years have passed since that event,

---

[1] The basement of St. Mary's Chapel continued to be open to the public till the death of Father A. Elder, in 1871.

Rt. Rev. B. J. Flaget, D. D.,
Bishop of Bardstown.

but the influence once exercised on the Community by old St. Mary's remains, and the roll of its two hundred and forty graduates and other pupils to-day exhibits a galaxy of honorable and useful citizens in every walk of life. Business men, bankers, doctors, lawyers, judges, writers, engineers, governors, and statesmen, many of them indeed are gone, but their survivors still cherish for their Alma Mater a deep interest, a tender love, a sort of college patriotism. Selecting only a few out of the long list, we have such names as ROBERT WALSH, A. B. ROMAN, the LATROBES, the CARROLLS, the JENKINS, the FOLEYS, S. ECCLESTON, J. J. CHANCHE, D. W. BACON, JOHN HOSKYNS, W. A. BLENKINSOP, FERDINAND E. CHATARD, CHARLES I. WHITE, S. T. WALLIS, ROBERT M. McLANE, EDWARD A. KNIGHT, CLEMENT C. BIDDLE, JOHN A. GARESCHÉ, REVERDY JOHNSON, JR.. WILLIAM T. MERRICK, BOLIVAR DANELS, ODEN BOWIE, FRANCIS E. BOYLE, LEO KNOTT, T. E. HAMBLETON, CHRISTOPHER JOHNSTON, CHARLES O'DONOVAN, DENNIS McKEW, JACOB A. WALTER, J. J. DOUGHERTY.

After the suppression of the College, the buildings were modified in order to accommodate the students of philosophy and theology. The house on the right hand side of St. Mary's Court, Pennsylvania Avenue, which heretofore had been used by the seminarians, was restricted to philosophy, whereas the buildings on the left, which had served for the College, were now occupied by the students of theology. The seminarians were no longer diverted from their studies and other sacred duties by foreign occupations, but vied with one another in holy emulation.

Their number increased rapidly and swelled the ranks of the clergy. Whilst the number of priests from 1791 to 1849 had been only one hundred and fourteen, from 1850 to 1861 there were one hundred and twelve, belonging to twenty-six dioceses. Among these we may recall the names of Richard Phelan, now Bishop of Pittsburg, Lawrence McMahon, Bishop of Hartford, John Foley, Bishop of Detroit, Patrick O'Reilly, Bishop of Springfield, Massachusetts, Michael McCabe, V. G., John T. Sullivan (Mgr.), Michael Moran, Edmund Didier, John Gloyd, John Gaitley, and JAMES GIBBONS, Cardinal Archbishop of Baltimore. Such a harvest rejoiced the exact but good-hearted Superior, Father Lhomme, who gently went to rest in the Lord in the year 1860. His successor was the Rev. Joseph Paul Dubreul, who, for the ten years previous, had discharged with success the duties of teacher or treasurer in the Seminary. A man of good business abilities, he kept up and increased the credit of St. Mary's during the crisis of the Civil War, and other financial troubles. Under his administration of eighteen years, the Institution continued to gain in prestige, and rose from thirty-five to ninety-two students. Among the professors of that period now gone to their reward, none reflected so much credit on the Seminary as the Rev. Alphonse Flammant, who taught from 1856 to 1864. Whilst his superior abilities, the depth and clearness of his teaching, excited the students' admiration, the suavity of his disposition won their hearts. Many were those who distinguished themselves under the eyes of their professors, and gave early promise of the services they are now rendering. The most conspicuous of these were J. J. Keane, the Right Rev. Rector of the Washington University; J. J. Kain, Bishop of Wheeling; J. O'Sullivan, Bishop of Mobile; A. A. Curtis, Bishop of Wilmington, Delaware; P. L. Chapelle, Coadjutor Bishop of Santa Fé; T. Griffin (Mgr.), D. J. O'Connell, Rt. Rev. Rector of the American College in Rome; T. M. A. Burke, V. G.; M. S. Gross, V. G.; J. M. McDermott, V. G.; D. O'Callaghan; C. T. McGrath; P. Murphy, S. T. L.; W. E. Starr; G. W. Devine; J. S. Duffy; T. F. Ward; R. J. Johnson; I. Zeller; P. J. McNamara; C. Reilly, D. D.; C. B. Rex, D. D. It was during this period (1869) that the saintly Father Jenkins went to his reward. He had presided at the laborious beginning of the Preparatory College of St. Charles, and had devoted to that Institution his life and his fortune. Success crowned his efforts, and the spirit of piety reigned in his community. He had actually founded a nursery of priests; and, when his summons came, the impulse that he had given to the good work was not slackened.

The crowning achievement in the career of Father Dubreul was the rearing of the present Seminary buildings on Paca St., which, with their modern improvements, became comfortable substitutes for the old edifices. The change marked an era in the history of St. Sulpice in Baltimore, though Father Dubreul was not destined to witness it. He died of pneumonia in the spring of 1878, and was succeeded in his office by the present incumbent, the Very Rev. A. Magnien, D. D.

Under the new superior there was an influx of candidates, which necessitated a separate Department of philosophy under a special Superior; and, subsequently, a double course of divinity. The large increase of students of philosophy, in the Fall of 1890, led to the erection of the North Western wing, which completes the original plan of the building.

The most notable event in the whole history of the Seminary occurred in the Autumn of 1885, when the Fathers of the Third Plenary Council held their sessions within its walls. The Exercise Hall was appropriated to that purpose, and decorated with the superb painting of Pope Leo XIII, who presided over the august assembly by his legate apostolic, his Eminence Cardinal Gibbons.

In concluding this imperfect and very incomplete sketch of St. Mary's Seminary during the past hundred years, we cannot refrain from expressing our earnest admiration for those self-sacrificing workers who *bore the burden of the day and the burning heat*, who broke the ground from which their successors reap. "*Others have labored, and ye have entered into their labors.*"

ST. MARY'S SEMINARY CHAPEL,
Dedicated 1808.

SUPERIORS OF ST. MARY'S SEMINARY.

VERY REV. FRANÇOIS CHARLES NAGOT, S. S. 1791–1810

VERY REV. MARIE JEAN TESSIER, S. S 1810–1829

VERY REV. LOUIS RÉGIS DELUOL, S. S. 1829–1849

VERY REV. FRANÇOIS LHOMME, S. S 1850–1860

VERY REV. JOSEPH PAUL DUBREUL, S. S 1860–1878

VERY REV. ALPHONSE MAGNIEN, S. S 1878–

PRESIDENTS OF ST. MARY'S COLLEGE.

Rev. W. DUBOURG, S. S.	1800–1810
	1811–1812
Rev. J. B. DAVID, S. S., *pro tem*	1810–1811
Rev. J. B. T. PAQUIET	1812–1815
Rev. S. BRUTÉ, S. S.	1815–1818
Rev. E. DAMPHOUX, S. S.	1818–1822
	1823–1827
	1828–1829
Rev. L. DELUOL, S. S	1822–1823
Rev. M. WHEELER, S. S	1827–1828
Rev. S. ECCLESTON, S. S.	1829–1834
Rev. J. J. CHANCHE, S. S	1835–1840
Rev. G. N. RAYMOND, S. S	1841–1849
Rev. O. L. JENKINS, S. S.	1850–1852

PROFESSORS OF ST. MARY'S SEMINARY.

Rev.	Jean Marie Tessier, S. S.	1791–1810
"	Antoine Garnier, S. S.	1791–1803
"	Michel Levadoux, S. S.	{ 1791–1792 1802–1803
"	Jean Baptiste Chicoisneau, S. S.	1792–1796
"	Jean Baptiste David, S. S.	1804–1811
"	Benoit Flaget, S. S.	1799–1809
"	Ambroise Maréchal, S. S.	{ 1792–1803 1812–1817
"	Louis Régis Deluol, S. S.	1817–1829
"	François Lhomme, S. S.	1827–1850
"	Augustin Vérot, S. S.	1830–1853
"	Pierre Frédet, S. S.	1831–1854
"	Joseph Paul Dubreul, S. S.	1850–1860
"	Stanislas Ferté, S. S.	1852–1869
"	Hyacinthe Roussel, S. S.	1854–1855
"	J. M. Gervais, S. S.	1855–1857
"	Alphonse Flammant, S. S.	1856–1864
"	François Paulin Dissez, S. S.	1857–
"	Urbain Lequerré, S. S.	1860–1871
"	Pierre Paul Chapon, S. S.	1863–1884
"	Sébastien Guilbaud, S. S.	1864–1869
"	Louis Rincé, S. S.	1869–1869
"	Alphonse Magnien, S. S.	1869–1878
"	Julien Dujarié, S. S.	1869–1871
"	Louis François Dumont, S. S.	{ 1871–1872 1880–1886
"	James McCallen, S. S.	{ 1871–1880 1881–1887
"	Auguste Fonteneau, S. S.	1872–1880

Rev. Gabriel André, S. S.		1878–1889
" Arsène Boyer, S. S.		1879–
" Clément Palin d'Abonville, S. S.		1880–1884
" Pierre Hamon, S. S.		1880–1882
" Edward R. Dyer, S. S.		1884–
" Joseph Haüg, S. S.		1884–1885
" Mathurin Rothureau, S. S.		1886–
" Eugène Forest, S. S.		1886–
" Adolphe A. Tanquerey, S. S.		1887–
" Edward A. L. Duffy		1887–1889
" Auguste M. Chéneau, S. S.		1889–
" Joseph V. Tracy		1889–
" Léon Besnard, S. S.		1890–
" Hippolyte L. Pluchon, S. S.		1890–

TEACHERS, TUTORS AND OTHER OFFICERS OF ST. MARY'S COLLEGE.

Rev. A. Garnier, S. S.	1800–1801
" P. Babade, S. S.	1800–1820
" J. M. Tessier, S. S.	1800–1801
Mr. Guillemin	1800–1801
" Dormenon	1801–1805
" Aymé	1801–1802
Rev. B. Flaget, S. S.	1802–1808
" J. B. T. Paquiet	1802–1812
Mr. Favrin	1804–1805
Rev. J. B. David, S. S.	1805–1806 / 1810–1811
Mr. Pechillou	1805–1806
" Marye	1805–1806
" A. De Mun	1805–1806
" J. Bergerac	1805–1810
" Shewads	1805–1806
" Mullon	1805–1807
" De Chevigné	1806–1825
" Duclairac	1806–1809
" T. Trigant	1806–1807
" Graham	1806–1807
" Tessandier	1806–1816
" B. Schipper	1806–1807
" Noinville	1806–1807
" Brunelot	1807–1810
" P. Woods	1807–1810
" V. Girard	1807–1808
" Hupfeld	1807–1809

Mr. Dupuy	1807-1808
Rev. J. Sinnot	1808-1823
Mr. A. Woolff	1808-1809
" J. B. Couret	1808-1809
" F. B. Moreau	1808-1810
Rev. H. Joubert, S. S.	1809-1852
Mr. Aigster	1809-1810
" A. Dubourg	1809-1810
" E. Fenwick	1809-1810
" B. Fenwick	1809-1810
" J. Crouzat	1809-1810
" M. Godefroy	1809-1818
Rev. S. Bruté, S. S.	1810-1812
" Carr	1810-1811
Mr. C. Joubert	1810-1819
" Comte	1810-1811
" Cazeaux	1810-1811
Rev. H. Xaupi, S. S.	1810-1827
" J. J. Chanche, S. S.	1811-1834
Mr. Brunelot	1811-1817
Rev. J. H. Hickey, S. S.	1812-1818 / 1826-1844
" A. Maréchal, S. S.	1813-1814 / 1816-1817
" E. Damphoux, S. S.	1813-1818 / 1822-1823
" H. Harent, S. S.	1813-1818
" N. Kerney,	1813-1818 / 1820-1823 / 1824-1825
Mr. Nenninger	1814-1823
" Nenninger, Jr.	1815-1839
" W. Byrne	1816-1819
" Bullet	1816-1819
" L. Geauty	1816-1818
Rev. A. Elder, S. S.	1816-1852
Mr. Doyle	1817-1818
Rev. L. Deluol, S. S.	1818-1849
" F. Vespré	1818-1819
" J. Randanne, S. S.	1818-1852

Most Rev. Ambrose Maréchal, D. D.,
Third Archbishop of Baltimore.

TEACHERS, ETC., OF ST. MARY'S COLLEGE.

Mr.	N. V. Boudet	1818–1819
Rev.	G. Shoenfelder	1818–1819
"	M. Wheeler, S. S	1818–1823 / 1828–1832
Mr.	C. Delacey	1818–1819
"	J. Commisky	1818–1819
Rev.	S. Eccleston, S. S.	1818–1825 / 1827–1834
Mr.	F. G. Forster	1819–1831
"	Anduze	1819–1820
"	McCready	1819–1820
"	Pise	1819–1820
"	McGione	1819–1820
"	McCosker	1819–1822
"	De Butts	1820–1821
"	Reynaud	1820–1822
"	McGowen	1820–1821
"	McGerry	1820–1821
"	Rafferty	1820–1821
"	A. Seghers	1820–1821
"	Samuel Smith	1820–1851
"	Mariano Cubi y Soner	1821–1828
"	W. Castel	1822–1825
"	Deagle	1822–1825
"	H. B. Coskrey	1823–1824 / 1833–1836
"	McGerry	1823–1824
"	Vanorsigh	1823–1824
"	Wm. T. Kelly	1823–1852
"	Jamieson	1823–1824
"	G. Carrell	1824–1825
Rev.	E. Knight, S. S.	1825–1851
Mr.	C. White	1825–1826
"	Owings	1825–1826
"	E. D. Genault	1825–1826
"	Williams	1826–1827
"	J. Larkin, S. S	1826–1827
"	Schriver	1826–1827
Rev.	F. Lhomme, S. S.	1827–1852
Mr.	M. S. Galligher	1827–1834

Rev. J. H. Hoskins, S. S.		1827-1836
Mr. H. J. Myers		1827-1836
" H. Dickehutt		1828-1829 / 1831-1833
" Guildeau		1828-1829
" Holmes		1828-1829
" Reily		1828-1829
" Gordon		1828-1829
" T. Hermange		1829-1830
Rev. A. Verot, S. S		1830-1852
Mr. J. A. Pizarro		1830-1852
Rev. H. Griffin		1832-1852
Mr. Penci		1832-1833
Rev. J. Lesne		1833-1834
" P. Fredet, S. S.		1833-1852
" S. B. Piot, S. S.		1833-1836
Mr. H. Burgess		1833-1836
" J. P. Donelan		1833-1836
" E. J. Chaisty		1833-1836
" M. Walsh		1833-1836
" J. Strain		1833-1836
" H. H. Colburn		1833-1836
" C. McManus		1835-1836
" A. Williamson		1836-1841
" D. W. Bacon		1834-1837
" H. J. Murphy		1834-1837
" P. Plunket		1834-1837
" H. J. Bogue		1834-1838
" E. J. Elder		1834-1838
" E. Friederici		1834-1838
" J. Dolan		1836-1841
" J. Murphy		1836-1843
" J. Lakenan		1836-1842
" J. B. Donelan		1836-1850
Rev. G. N. Raymond		1838-1841
Mr. E. McColgan		1838-1839
" J. Hewitt		1838-1842
" H. A. Allen		1839-1852
" W. A. Blenkinsop		1839-1844
" J. J. Maguire		1839-1850

TEACHERS, ETC., OF ST. MARY'S COLLEGE. 45

Mr.	P. J. Fitzsimmons	1839–1840
"	A. Frietag	1839–1852
"	A. Calder	1840–1842
"	F. Brunet	1841–1843
Rev.	B. Bayer	1841–1842
Mr.	P. Courtney	1841–1843
Rev.	T. P. Foley	1841–1847
Mr.	C. T. Keenan	1841–1843
"	M. Slattery	1841–1847
Rev.	H. Murphy	1842–1843
Mr.	F. X. Brunet	1842–1843
Rev.	O. L. Jenkins, S. S.	1842–1848
Mr.	J. B. Donelan	1842–1844
"	M. Oertel	1843–1844
"	A. Bazire	1843–1845
"	T. G. Riordon	1843–1850
"	W. Parsons	1843–1850
"	C. C. Brennan	1843–1845
Rev.	C. I. White	1844–1846
Mr.	E. McNerhany	1844–1847
"	J. Norris	1844–1848
"	F. King	1845–1848
"	P. Dalton	1845–1848
"	H. S. Hennis	1845–1850
"	J. Lawrence	1846–1850
"	F. Boyle	1847–1850
"	J. Dougherty	1848–1852
"	T. W. McCleery	1848–1852
"	B. J. McManus	1848–1850
"	J. McNally	1848–1851
"	S. Huber	1848–1850
"	F. Jenkins	1848–1850
"	B. Belt	1848–1850
"	E. P. Wadhams	1848–1850
Rev.	J. P. Dubreul, S. S.	1850–1852
"	M. Feller, S. S.	1850–1851
Mr.	Edw. O'Brien	1850–1851
"	H. F. Parke	1850–1851
"	J. Cunningham	1850–1851
"	C. F. McDonald	1850–1851

SEMINARY OF ST. SULPICE.

Mr.	F. X. Leray	1850-1852
"	A. McDonald	1850-1851
"	J. H. Walters	1850-1852
"	J. Carney	1850-1852
"	A. L. Knott	1851-1852
"	A. McDonnell	1851-1852
"	J. Farran	1851-1852
"	J. Mulligan	1851-1852
"	Jas. Doyle	1851-1852
"	A. Van Schalkuyck	1851-1852
"	C. E. Gephard	1851-1852
Rev.	C. M. E. Voirdye	1851-1852

REV. O. L. JENKINS,
First President of St. Charles' College.

SULPICIANS AT ST. CHARLES' COLLEGE, MT. ST. MARY'S, AND IN THE MISSIONS.

AT ST. CHARLES' COLLEGE, ELLICOTT CITY, MD.

Rev. O. L. Jenkins	....	{ 1848-1849 1852-1869
" G. N. Raymond [1]	....	1849-1851
" J. B. Menu	....	1849-1888
" S. Ferté	....	{ 1851-1852 1869-1876
" J. B. Randanne	....	1852-1864
" P. Frédet	....	1854-1855
" R. Blanc	....	1856-1860
" H. M. Chapuis	....	1857-
" P. P. Denis	....	1860-
" P. Deguire	....	1860-1860
" J. T. Parent	....	1860-1862
" S. Guilbaud	....	{ 1861-1865 1869-
" G. E. Viger	....	1862-
" L. Rincé	....	1862-1869
" J. Dujarié	....	1864-1869
" F. L. M. Dumont [2]	....	{ 1865-1871 1872-1880 1886-
" A. J. B. Vuibert	....	1865-
" M. Vignon	....	1865-1875
" A. S. Fonteneau	....	{ 1868-1872 1880-

[1] Left the Society and exercised the ministry in Louisiana, where he died in 1880.
[2] The present President of the College.

47

SEMINARY OF ST. SULPICE.

Rev.	C. Schrantz	1871–
"	C. J. Judge	1876–
"	P. F. Roux	1877–1885 / 1888–
"	J. Haug	1879–1880 / 1885–
"	J. A. McCallen	1880–1881
"	R. K. Wakeham	1881–
"	C. B. Rex	1883–1884
"	F. X. McKenny	1884–1885 / 1890–
"	A. P. Bernard	1885–1886 / 1888–
Mr.	D. E. Maher	1886–1887
Rev.	G. C. Clapin	1887–1888
"	A. M. Chéneau	1887–1889
Mr.	D. E. Duffy	1887–1888
Rev.	P. C. Dumont	1888–1890

IN MT. ST. MARY'S COLLEGE, EMMITSBURG.

Rev.	J. Dubois[1]	1808–1826
"	S. G. Bruté[2]	1812–1815 / 1818–1834
"	John Hickey	1814–1818 / 1826–1844

IN THE UNITED STATES MISSIONS.

Rev. M. Levadoux,[3]
" J. B. David,[4]
" B. Flaget,[5]
" Father Ciquard,
" D. de Galitzin,
" John Dilhet,[6]
" G. I. Chabrat.[7]

[1] Consecrated Bishop of New York in 1826; died in 1842.
[2] Bishop of Vincennes in 1834; died in 1839.
[3] He was employed in the Illinois missions from 1792 to 1802.
[4] Consecrated Coadjutor Bishop of Bardstown in 1819.
[5] Consecrated Bishop of Bardstown in 1810.
[6] He worked with zeal in the Illinois missions from 1798 to 1806.
[7] Consecrated Coadjutor Bishop of Bardstown in 1836.

VERY REV. MARIE JEAN TESSIER,
Second Superior of the Seminary.

STUDENTS OF ST. MARY'S SEMINARY THAT HAVE BEEN ORDAINED PRIESTS.

The Seminary will be under obligations to any reader sending notice of inaccuracies or omissions in the following lists.

NAMES.	DIOCESES.	ORDAINING PRELATES.	YEARS OF ORDINAT.
BADIN, STEPH. T.	Baltimore.	Rt. Rev. J. Carroll.	1793
PERRINEAU, PETER J.[1]	Quebec.	?	1793 or 94
GALITZIN, DEM. A.	Baltimore.	Rt. Rev. J. Carroll.	1795
FLOYD, JOHN.	"	" "	"
DE MONTDÉSIR, J. E.	"	" "	1798
MATTHEWS, W.	"	" "	1800
BROOKE, IGNATIUS.	"	" "	1801
MONEREAU, D.	"	" "	1802
CUDDY, M.	"	" "	1803
DE PERRIGNY, G.	"	" "	"
ROLOFF, FR.	"	" "	1808
O'BRIEN, WILLIAM.	"	" "	"
FENWICK, BENED. J.[2]	"	Rt. Rev. L. Neale.	"
FENWICK, ENOCH.	"	" "	"
SPINK, JAMES.	"	" "	"
EDELEN, LEONARD.	"	" "	"
BYRNE, MICHAEL.	"	Rt. Rev. J. Carroll.	1809
JOUBERT, JACQUES.	"	" "	1810
MARSHALL, JOHN.	"	Rt. Rev. L. Neale.	1811

[1] Was ordained at Quebec either by the bishop of that city, Rt. Rev. Fr. Hubert, or by his coadjutor, Rt. Rev. Dr. Bailly.

[2] The second Bishop of Boston. He, the three following, and John Marshall, joined the Society of Jesus before being ordained.

SEMINARY OF ST. SULPICE.

NAMES.	DIOCESES.	ORDAINING PRELATES.	YEARS OF ORDINAT.
Chabrat, Ignatius.[1]	Bardstown.	Rt. Rev. B. J. Flaget.	1811
Derigaud, Jacques.	"	" "	"
Harent, Joseph.	Baltimore.	Mt. Rev. J. Carroll.	1812*
deClorivière, Jos. P.	"	" "	"
Moynihan, James.	"	" "	1813
Damphoux, Edw.	"	" "	1814
Hickey, John.	"	" "	"
Schaeffer, Peter.	Bardstown.	Rt. Rev. B. J. Flaget.	"
Smith, Roger M.	Baltimore.	Mt. Rev. J. Carroll.	1815
Carroll, Denis.	Philadelphia.	?	"
O'Connor, Patrick.	Baltimore.	Mt. Rev. L. Neale.	"
Hollands, John.	Philadelphia.	Rt. Rev. J. de Cheverus.	1816
Cooper, Samuel.	Baltimore.	Mt. Rev. A. Maréchal.	1818†
Kearney, Nicholas.	"	" "	"
Fairclough, Jos. W.	"	" "	"
Sheinfelder, Geo.	Philadelphia.	" "	"
Xaupi, H. X.	Baltimore.	" "	1819
Chanche, John J.[2]	"	" "	"
O'Brien, Timothy.	"	" "	"
Byrne, William.	Bardstown.	Rt. Rev. B. J. Flaget.	"
Elder, George.	"	" "	"
Cummiskey, James.	Baltimore.	Mt. Rev. A. Maréchal.	1820
Hogan, Geo. D.	Philadelphia.	" "	"
Elder, Al. J.	Baltimore.	" "	"
Wheeler, Mich. F.	"	" "	"
Anduze, Matth. B.	New Orleans.	Rt. Rev. W. Dubourg.	1821
Heyden, Thomas.	Philadelphia.	Rt. Rev. H. Conwell.	"
Dwen, Patrick I.	"	" "	"

1 Second coadjutor of Bishop Flaget.
2 First Bishop of Natchez.

* *Note.*—In that year, Anth. Deydier was ordained a deacon. He afterwards taught for four years at Mt. St. Mary's refusing to receive the priesthood, and subsequently was a private tutor in the neighborhood of Albany. In 1838 he appears for the first time in the Catholic Directory as a priest of the diocese of Vincennes. Probably he had been ordained by Bishop Bruté who had known him at the Mountain.

† *Note.*—In that year Francis Vespre, a St. Mary's Seminarian, from March, 1813, to November, 1818, left for Rome for the purpose of joining the Society of Jesus. In the Catholic directory of 1840, he is mentioned as being at Georgetown College procurator of the Province.

REV. STEPHEN T. BADIN,
The first Priest ordained in the U. S., May 25th, 1793.

Rev. Demetrius A. Galitzin.

STUDENTS THAT HAVE BEEN ORDAINED.

NAMES.	DIOCESES.	ORDAINING PRELATES.	YEARS OF ORDINAT.
DELANEY, CHRISTOPH.	Richmond.	Rt. Rev. P. Kelly.	1821
RAFFERTY, PATRICK.	Philadelphia.	Rt. Rev. H. Conwell.	1822
REYNOLDS, IGNAT. A.[1]	Bardstown.	Mt. Rev. A. Maréchal.	1823
McCOSKER, FERD.	Baltimore.	Mt. Rev. A. Maréchal.	1824
McGERRY, JOHN.	"	" " "	"
VAN HORSIGH, JOS.	"	" " "	"
PISE, CHARLES.	"	" " "	1825
ECCLESTON, SAMUEL.[2]	"	" " "	"
HOERNER, JAMES.	"	" " "	1826
DEAGLE, MATT. P.	"	" " "	"
KENNY, ANTHONY.	"	" " "	"
CARRELL, GEORGE A.[3]	Philadelphia.	Rt. Rev. H. Conwell.	"
SCHREIBER, P. S.	Baltimore.	Mt. Rev. A. Maréchal.	1827
LARKIN, JOHN A.	"	" " "	"
GILDEA, JOHN B.	"	Mt. Rev. Jas. Whitfield.	1829
JAMISON, FRANCIS.	"	" " "	"
KNIGHT, EDWARD.	"	" " "	1830
FLAUT, GEORGE.	"	" " "	"
WHITE, CHARLES.	"	Mt. Rev. H. de Quelen.	"
MYERS, HENRY.	"	Mt. Rev. Jas. Whitfield.	1831
HOSKYNS, JOHN.	"	" " "	1832
CARTER, CHARLES J.	Philadelphia.	Rt. Rev. F. P. Kenrick.	"
PIOT, BERTRAND.	Baltimore.	Mt. Rev. Sam. Eccleston.	1833
COSKERY, HENRY.	"	" " "	1834
McGILL, JOHN.[4]	Bardstown.	Rt. Rev. B. J. Flaget.	"
STARRS, WILLIAM.	New York.	Rt. Rev. J. Dubois.	"
DONELAN, JOHN P.	Baltimore.	Mt. Rev. Sam. Eccleston.	1836
GALLIGHER, MICH.	"	" " "	"
HEAS, MICHAEL.	New York.	" " "	1837
BENOIT, JULIEN.	Vincennes.	Rt. Rev. S. G. Bruté.	"
STRAIN, JAMES.	Baltimore.	Mt. Rev. Sam. Eccleston.	"
CORRY, PATRICK.	"	" " "	"

[1] Second Bishop of Charleston.
[2] The fifth Archbishop of Baltimore.
[3] First Bishop of Covington.
[4] Third Bishop of Richmond.

SEMINARY OF ST. SULPICE.

NAMES.	DIOCESES.	ORDAINING PRELATES.	YEARS OF ORDINAT.
OBERMEYER, LEON A.	Baltimore.	Mt. Rev. Sam. Eccleston.	1837
MCCAFFREY, JOHN H.	"	" "	1838
MCCAFFREY, THOS.	"	" "	"
GRIFFIN, HUGH F.	"	" "	"
BACON, DAVID WM.[1]	New York.	" "	"
MCCOLGAN, EDWARD.	Baltimore.	" "	1839
DOLAN, JAMES JOS.	"	" "	1840
LOUGHLIN, JOHN.[2]	New York.	Rt. Rev. J. Dubois.	"
MURPHY, HENRY.	Baltimore.	Mt. Rev. Sam. Eccleston.	1842
COURTNEY, PATRICK.	"	" "	"
DONELAN, JAMES B.	"	" "	"
BLENKINSOP, WM. A.	"	" "	1843
MAGUIRE, JOSEPH.	"	Mt. Rev. Sam. Eccleston.	1844
SLATTERY, MICHAEL.	"	" "	"
JENKINS, OLIVER L.	"	" "	"
BRENNAN, CHAS. C.	"	" "	"
PARSONS, WILLIAM D.	"	" "	1845
FOLEY, THOMAS P.[3]	"	" "	1846
KING, FRANCIS.	"	" "	1847
DALTON, PATRICK.	"	" "	"
LAWRENCE, ROB. JAS.	Wheeling.	" "	1848
CATON, EDWARD.	Baltimore.	" "	1849
LENAGHAN, PETER B.	"	" "	"
LAMBERT, WILLIAM.	Pittsburg.	" "	"
LARKIN, JOHN.	"	" "	"
WADHAMS, EDGAR P.[4]	Albany.	Rt. Rev. J. McCloskey.	"
O'BRIEN, EDWARD J.	Hartford.	Mt. Rev. Sam. Eccleston.	1850
MCMANUS, BERN. J.	Baltimore.	" "	"
PARKE, H. F.	Wheeling.	Rt. Rev. R. Whelan.	"
ARDOIS, CLEM. D.	Natchez.	Rt. Rev. J. J. Chanche.	1851
LERAY, FR. X.[5]	"	" "	"
MCNALLY, JOHN J.	Baltimore.	Mt. Rev. Sam. Eccleston.	"

[1] First Bishop of Portland.
[2] The first and present Bishop of Brooklyn.
[3] Bishop Administrator of Chicago from 1870 to 1879.
[4] The first and present Bishop of Ogdensburg.
[5] Fourth Archbishop of New Orleans.

STUDENTS THAT HAVE BEEN ORDAINED. 53

NAMES.	DIOCESES.	ORDAINING PRELATES.	YEARS OF ORDINAT.
BOYLE, FR. EDWARD.	Baltimore.	Mt. Rev. Sam. Eccleston.	1851
TRACY, JAMES.	Pittsburg.	Mt. Rev. F. P. Kenrick.	1852
O'FARRELL, THOS.	Buffalo.	Rt. Rev. J. Timon.	"
COADY, JOHN.	Pittsburg.	Rt. Rev. M. O'Connor.	"
HENNIS, H. E. S.	Boston.	Rt. Rev. Ig. Bourget.	"
DOUGHERTY, JOHN.	Baltimore.	Mt. Rev. F. P. Kenrick.	1853
CARNEY, JAMES.	"	" " "	"
CUNNINGHAM, JAS. V.	Wheeling.	Rt. Rev. R. Whelan.	"
WALTERS, J. H.	"	" " "	"
GIBBONS, DOMINIC.	Mobile.	Rt. Rev. M. Portier.	"
WALTER, JACOB A.	Baltimore.	Mt. Rev. F. P. Kenrick.	1854
MARSOLAIS, PIERRE.	Montreal.	Rt. Rev. Ig. Bourget.	"
FARRAN, JOHN C.	Pittsburg.	Rt. Rev. M. O'Connor.	"
CHRISTY, RICHARD.	"	" " "	"
PHELAN, RICHARD.[1]	"	" " "	"
CODY, PETER.	Hartford.	Rt. Rev. B. O'Reilly.	"
MCCALLION, MICH.	"	" " "	"
DUFFY, WILLIAM.	"	" " "	"
MCCABE, MICHAEL R.	"	" " "	"
CARROLL, MATTHEW.	Pittsburg.	Rt. Rev. M. O'Connor.	1855
O'BRANIGAN, K.	"	" " "	"
CONWAY, PATRICK.	Toronto.	Rt. Rev. A. de Charbonnel.	"
MCMAHON, PETER.	Covington.	Rt. Rev. G. A. Carrell.	"
VEHRLÉ, MARY P.	Detroit.	Rt. Rev. P. P. Lefévre.	"
DURNING, DANIEL G.	New York.	Rt. Rev. J. Hughes.	"
LYMAN, EDWARD D.	Baltimore.	Mt. Rev. F. P. Kenrick.	1856
O'CONNER, DANIEL.	Wheeling.	Rt. Rev. R. Whelan.	"
FOLEY, JOHN S.[2]	Baltimore.	His Em. Card. Patrizi.	"
MORAN, MICHAEL.	Boston.	Rt. Rev. D. W. Bacon.	1857
O'REILLY, PATR. T.[3]	"	" " "	"
HARTNEY, MICHAEL.	"	" " "	"
MEUFFELS, HENRY.	Detroit.	Rt. Rev. P. P. Lefévre.	"
SULLIVAN, JOHN T.	Wheeling.	Rt. Rev. G. A. Carrell.	"
BRANDTS, E. H.	Covington.	" " "	"

[1] The present Bishop of Pittsburg.
[2] The present Bishop of Detroit.
[3] The first and present Bishop of Springfield (Mass.).

SEMINARY OF ST. SULPICE.

NAMES.	DIOCESES.	ORDAINING PRELATES.	YEARS OF ORDINAT.
Dugluet, Joseph M.	Burlington.	Rt. Rev. L. de Goesbriand.	1857
Boubat, Barth.	London (Canada).	Rt. Rev. P. A. Pinsonneault	"
Sauvadet, Andre.	"	"	"
Michel, Joseph.	Toronto.	Rt. Rev. A. de Charbonnel.	"
De Saunhac, Paul.	Hamilton.	Rt. Rev. J. Farrell.	"
Bardou, Pierre.	"	"	"
Carroll, William.	Albany.	Rt. Rev. J. McCloskey.	"
O'Hara, James.	"	"	"
Keveny, Philip.	"	"	"
Cassidy, Stephen.	Brooklyn.	Rt. Rev. J. Loughlin.	"
Brennan, Edward.	Baltimore.	Mt. Rev. F. P. Kenrick.	1858
McDevitt, James.	"	"	"
Didier, Edmund.	"	"	"
Gloyd, John C.	"	"	"
English, Dennis.	Buffalo.	"	"
Hergenroether, C.	C. S. S. R.	"	"
Cloarec, J. M.	Burlington.	Rt. Rev. L. de Goesbriand.	"
McGlynn, Patrick.	Albany.	Rt. Rev. J. McCloskey.	"
Hogan, James.	"	"	"
Tixier, Marius.	Toronto.	Rt. Rev. A. de Charbonnel.	"
Laurent, Peter.	"	"	"
Braire, Louis.	"	"	"
Guillon, Mich. A.	"	"	"
O'Shea, Michael.	"	"	"
Tuohy, James.	Buffalo.	Rt. Rev. J. Timon.	"
Malloy, Laurence.	Baltimore.	Mt. Rev. F. P. Kenrick.	1859
McCosker, Ed.	Newark.	"	"
Bohen, James.	Hartford.	"	"
Mullen, Daniel.	"	"	"
Coit, Bernard B.	"	"	"
Michel, Andrew.	Covington.	Rt. Rev. G. A. Carrell.	"
Byrne, Patrizio.	Buffalo.	Rt. Rev. J. Timon.	"
O'Mara, James.	"	"	"
Daly, Philip.	Hartford.	?	"
Mahoney, William.	Baltimore.	Mt. Rev. F. P. Kenrick.	1860
McCarthy, P. F.	Baltimore.	"	"
Fagan, John.	Hartford.	"	"

VERY REV. LOUIS RÉGIS DELUOL,
Third Superior of the Seminary.

STUDENTS THAT HAVE BEEN ORDAINED. 55

NAMES.	DIOCESES.	ORDAINING PRELATES.	YEARS OF ORDINAT.
CORRIGAN, P.	Newark.	Mt. Rev. F. P. Kenrick.	1860
BYRNE, PATRICK.	"	Rt. Rev. James Bailey.	"
HICKEY, EDWARD M.	"	" "	"
KOOPMANS, CHARLES.	Covington.	Rt. Rev. G. A. Carrell.	"
GERARD, JOSEPH.	London.	Rt. Rev. Ig. Bourget.	"
WAGNER, JAMES F.	"	" "	"
GIBBONS, JAMES.[1]	Baltimore.	Mt. Rev. F. P. Kenrick.	1861
GAITLEY, JOHN T.	"	" "	"
BIRCH, JOSEPH ST.	"	" "	"
HAGAN, JOHN P.	Richmond.	" "	"
FINUCANE, JOHN.	Natchez.	" "	"
CAMPBELL, JAMES F.	Hartford.	" "	"
REGNOUF, VICTOR.	V. A. Florida.	Rt. Rev. A. Verot.	"
O'REILLY, JAMES.	Hartford.	?	"
O'FARRELL, THOMAS.	Brooklyn.	Mt. Rev. F. P. Kenrick.	1862
MCDERMOTT, JAMES.	Albany.	Rt. Rev. J. McCloskey.	"
MCMAHON, LAUR. S.[2]	Boston.	His Em. Card. Patrizi.	"
CAISSY, NAPOL. G.	Burlington.	Rt. Rev. L. de Goesbriand.	"
DALY, WILLIAM J.	Boston.	Rt. Rev. Ig. Bourget.	"
BARRETT, JOHN AL.	Louisville.	?	"
FOLEY, CORNELIUS M.	Boston.	Mt. Rev. F. P. Kenrick.	1863
MALLON, HUGH.	Hartford.	" "	"
SHERRY, JAMES J.	Albany.	Rt. Rev. J. McCloskey.	"
BURKE, THOS. M. A.	Albany.	Rt. Rev. F. P. McFarland.	1864
ORR, WILLIAM.	Boston.	" "	"
MCCARTEN, JAMES.	Hartford.	" "	"
MCCURRY, FR. P.	Albany.	" "	"
SCHULTE, EBERH.	Covington.	" "	"
STEPHANY, JOHN.	"	" "	"
LEONARD, PATRICK.	Newark.	" "	"
SMITH, JOHN H.	Hartford.	" "	"
MCCABE, JOHN.	"	Mt. Rev. M. J. Spalding.	"
CASSIN, JOSEPH H.	Boston.	Rt. Rev. L. de Goesbriand.	"
HUSSEY, JOSEPH W.	New York.	" "	"

[1] The Card. Archbishop of Baltimore.
[2] The fifth and present Bishop of Hartford.

NAMES.	DIOCESES.	ORDAINING PRELATES.	YEARS OF ORDINAT.
TANDY, PATRICK.	New York.	Mt. Rev. J. McCloskey.	1864
FITZPATRICK, ED. IG.	St. Louis.	Mt. Rev. P. R. Kenrick.	"
HANNET, WILLIAM B.	London.	Rt. Rev. Ig. Bourget.	"
BAENSIGER, EDWARD.	Buffalo.	Rt. Rev. J. Timon.	"
CHAPELLE, L. P.[1]	Baltimore.	Mt. Rev. M. J. Spalding.	1865
BARRY, JOSEPH L.	"	" " "	"
JORDAN, WILLIAM L.	"	" " "	"
O'CALLAGHAN, DENIS.	Boston.	" " "	"
O'KEEFE, DENIS A.	"	" " "	"
GRACE, CH. F.	"	" " "	"
MCGRATH, CHRIST. T.	"	" " "	"
O'BRIEN, CORNELIUS.	Covington.	" " "	"
CRANE, EUGENE M.	Louisville.	Rt. Rev. P. J. Lavialle.	"
DALTON, JAMES F.	Newark.	Rt. Rev. James Baily.	"
MORAN, MICH. J. J.	Buffalo.	Rt. Rev. J. Timon.	"
KESSELER, ANTHONY.	New York.	Mt. Rev. J. McCloskey.	"
RYAN, NICHOLAS.	Louisville.	Rt. Rev. P. J. Lavialle.	"
MCNERNEY, JAMES.	Covington.	Rt. Rev. G. A. Carrell.	"
SHEA, MICHAEL JAS.	Boston.	?	"
O'BRIEN, MICHAEL.	Portland.	Rt. Rev. D. W. Bacon.	"
KEANE, JOHN J.[2]	Baltimore.	Mt. Rev. M. J. Spalding.	1866
MCCOY, PETER.	"	" " "	"
MORGAN, L. A.	"	" " "	"
VOLZ, HENRY.	"	" " "	"
KAIN, J. J.[3]	Richmond.	" " "	"
MCCABE, MICH. J.	St. Louis.	" " "	"
MCCABE, JAMES J.	"	" " "	"
SCHUCHART, JOHN M.	Covington.	" " "	"
DONOVAN, RICH. JOS.	Boston.	" " "	"
KAMMERER, GUST.	Brooklyn.	" " "	"
BRIC, WILLIAM.	Hartford.	" " "	"
LANE, WILLIAM.	Brooklyn.	" " "	"
MCDERMOTT, JAMES.	Albany.	Rt. Rev. J. McCloskey.	"
O'CONNELL, DANIEL.	"	Rt. Rev. J. J. Conroy.	"

[1] Bishop of Arabisso, Coadjutor of the Archbishop of Santa Fé.
[2] Bishop of Jasso, Rector of the Catholic University.
[3] Second and present Bishop of Wheeling.

STUDENTS THAT HAVE BEEN ORDAINED.

NAMES.	DIOCESES.	ORDAINING PRELATES.	YEARS OF ORDINAT.
SHIELDS, H. J.	Albany.	Rt. Rev. J. J. Conroy.	1866
MCSHERRY, EUGENE.	Brooklyn.	Rt. Rev. J. Loughlin.	"
DALY, PETER.	Newark.	Rt. Rev. Jas. Bailey.	"
WALSH, LAURENCE.	Hartford.	Rt. Rev. Ign. Bourget.	"
SMITH, H. P.	Boston.	?	"
MALONEY, PATRICK.	Erie.	?	"
HENDRICKS, JER.	Baltimore.	Rt. Rev. R. Whelan.	1867
QUINN, FRANCIS A.	Boston.	" "	"
DELAHUNTY, JOHN.	"	" "	"
GRIFFIN, THOMAS.	"	" "	"
FITZPATRICK, JER. ST.	Hartford.	" "	"
LAWLER, P. P.	"	" "	"
BAZIN, L. D.	Savannah.	" "	"
LINGS, A. A.	New York.	Rt. Rev. D. V. Bacon.	"
POLLARD, J. H.	Brooklyn.	?	"
RHATIGAN, LOUIS J.	"	?	"
FLYNN, JOHN S.	Hartford.	Rt. Rev. J. J. Conroy.	"
LOWERY, JOHN F.	Albany.	Rt. Rev. D. W. Bacon.	"
REILLY, CHARLES.	Newark.	Rt. Rev. James Bailey.	"
GAFFNEY, OWEN.	Hartford.	?	"
SHERIDAN, BARNEY.	"	?	"
RYAN, J. P.	Louisville.	Rt. Rev. J. H. Luers.	"
O'DONOVAN, D. J.	"	" "	"
KINTRUP, H. B.	Vincennes.	" "	"
KENNY, THOMAS H.	Boston.	Rt. Rev. D. W. Bacon.	"
CAREY, JAMES P.	Baltimore.	Mt. Rev. M. J. Spalding.	1868
MACKIN, JAMES F.	"	" "	"
O'SULLIVAN, JER.[1]	"	" "	"
SCHMITT, VAL. F.	"	" "	"
DUGGAN, F. P.	"	" "	"
RYAN, STANISLAS F.	"	" "	"
MURPHY, PAT'K F. A.	Hartford.	" "	"
GROSS, MARK S.[2]	V. A. N. Carolina.	" "	"
HEALEY, JER. J.	Boston.	" "	"

[1] The fourth and present Bishop of Mobile.
[2] In 1880 he was appointed Bishop and Vicar Apostolic of North Carolina, but he declined consecration after receipt of bulls and sent his resignation.

SEMINARY OF ST. SULPICE.

NAMES.	DIOCESES.	ORDAINING PRELATES.	YEARS OF ORDINAT.
Lennon, Fr.	Brooklyn.	Mt. Rev. M. J. Spalding.	1868
McElroy, James.	"	" "	"
Zeller, Ignatius H.	"	" "	"
Fagan, John.	"	" "	"
Borg, B. T.	Fort Wayne.	" "	"
Meissner, H.	"	" "	"
Dolan, Michael.	Boston.	" "	"
McGurk, James J.	Richmond.	" "	"
Flatley, Michael F.	Boston.	" "	"
Quinn, Nicholas J.	Albany.	Rt. Rev. J. J. Conroy.	"
Denoyel, Charles.	New Orleans.	Mt. Rev. J. M. Odin.	"
Peyron, Clement.	Santa Fé.	Rt. Rev. J. B. Lamy.	"
Novert, Eugene.	"	" "	"
Chevalier, Pierre.	Natchez.	Rt. Rev. W. H. Elder.	"
Vally, Louis.	"	" "	"
De Morangies, H. M.	"	" "	"
O'Connor, J. J.	Newark.	Rt. Rev. Jas. Bailey.	"
McFaul, Daniel.	Portland.	Mt. Rev. M. J. Spalding.	1869
Starr, William E.	Baltimore.	" "	"
Damer, C.	"	" "	"
O'Brien, Wm. F.	Hartford.	" "	"
Fuchs, Laur.	Brooklyn.	" "	"
Schwarz, Peter.	"	" "	"
Coughlan, William.	Boston.	" "	"
Bré, Oliver.	New Orleans.	" "	"
Brunel, A.	"	" "	"
Magniny, T.	"	" "	"
Rouillard, H.	"	" "	"
Jouan, P. M.	"	Mt. Rev. J. M. Odin.	"
Keane, Michael.	St. Louis.	Mt. Rev. M. J. Spalding.	"
Garassu, R. A.	Santa Fé.	" "	"
Lestra, Francis.	"	Rt. Rev. J. B. Lamy.	"
Parisis, Stephen.	"	" "	"
Badoil, E. M.	New Orleans.	Mt. Rev. J. M. Odin.	"
Healey, Daniel.	Boston.	Mt. Rev. J. McCloskey.	"
Hugon, J. L.	Savannah.	Rt. Rev. A. Verot.	"
Halbedl, Matthew.	New Orleans.	Mt. Rev. J. M. Odin.	"

VERY REV. FRANCOIS LHOMME.
Fourth Superior of the Seminary.

STUDENTS THAT HAVE BEEN ORDAINED.

NAMES.	DIOCESES.	ORDAINING PRELATES.	YEARS OF ORDINAT.
LOSSOUARN, E. M.	New Orleans.	Mt. Rev. M. J. Spalding.	1869
MASSARDIER, P. M.	"	Mt. Rev. J. M. Odin.	"
HIGGINS, M. F.	Boston.	Mt. Rev. J. McCloskey.	"
LAMB, PATRICK FR.	"	?	"
HENNESSY, RICHARD.	Scranton.	Rt. Rev. Wm. O'Hara.	"
O'BRIEN, JAMES M.	Baltimore.	Rt. Rev. T. P. Foley.	1870
GALLEN, JOSEPH A.	"	" "	"
MCNAMARA, PAT'K J.	Brooklyn.	" "	"
HEFFERNAN, JAS. A.	"	" "	"
BLANC, FLOR.	Natchez.	" "	"
MCVEREY, J.	Richmond.	" "	"
CONATY, B.	Boston.	" "	"
VAUDRAY, T. A. A.	Chicago.	" "	"
JAEGERING, H.	St. Louis.	Rt. Rev. P. J. Baltes.	"
SCHMIDT, JOSEPH.	"	" "	"
REMUZON, J. J.	Santa Fe.	Rt. Rev. J. B. Lamy.	"
BOYSE, RICHARD.	Brooklyn.	Rt. Rev. J. Loughlin.	"
CAFFERTY, EDWARD.	Savannah.	Rt. Rev. A. Verot.	"
TOBIN, PATRICK G.	New Orleans.	Rt. Rev. C. M. Dubuis.	"
FLANAGAN, J. D.	" "	" "	"
MCCALLEN, JAMES A.	V. A. N. Carolina.	Rt.Rev.C.de laHailandière.	"
FINNIGAN, J. A.	Hartford.	?	"
MCCARTHY, L. P.	Boston.	Rt. Rev. L. F. Laflèche.	"
DEVINE, GEORGE W.	Baltimore.	Rt. Rev. Thos. A. Becker.	1871
HANDS, JOHN.	V. A. N. Carolina.	" "	"
MCKEEFRY, H. J.	Richmond.	" "	"
KELLY, MICHAEL F.	Hartford.	" "	"
MCELHINEY, J.	Brooklyn.	" "	"
FLEMING, H. P.	Newark.	" "	"
DUNN, E. J.	Chicago.	" "	"
JOHNSON, R. J.	Boston.	" "	"
RIBERA, JOSEPH.	Santa Fe.	Mt. Rev. J. B. Purcell.	"
LAMY, ANTH.	"	" "	"
MULLEN, J. J.	St. Paul.	Rt. Rev. Thos. L. Grace.	"
MULLEN, JOSEPH.	Wheeling.	Rt. Rev. R. Whelan.	"
BOLAND, JOHN B. F.	Boston.	Mt. Rev. Abp. Chalandon.	"
GUYOT, J. M.	Galveston.	Rt. Rev. C. M. Dubuis.	"

SEMINARY OF ST. SULPICE.

NAMES.	DIOCESES.	ORDAINING PRELATES.	YEARS OF ORDINAT.
Chandy, P. F.	Galveston.	Rt. Rev. C. M. Dubuis.	1871
Ozanne, L. P.	New Orleans.	Mt. Rev. N. J. Perché.	"
Bardi, M.	" "	" "	"
Perrad, L. M. E.	Lyons.	Mt. Rev. Abp. Ginoulhac.	"
Kuper, F.	St. Louis.	Rt. Rev. John Henni.	"
McMahon, Patrick.	Chicago.	Rt. Rev. T. P. Foley.	"
O'Connor, James A.	"	" "	"
Reilly, Michael T.	Savannah.	Rt. Rev. Jas. Gibbons.	1872
Donnelly, Richard.	Boston.	" "	"
Amman, J. J.	Brooklyn.	" "	"
Duffy, James S.	"	" "	"
Bohier, J. E.	"	" "	"
McCourt, Edw. P.	Springfield.	" "	"
Callery, P. F.	"	" "	"
O'Connor, F.	Chicago.	" "	"
Schmitt, Caspar.	Baltimore.	Rt. Rev. Th. Becker.	"
Delaney, John.	"	" "	"
Marx, B. A.	"	" "	"
Starkey, J. T.	"	" "	"
Forhan, Michael.	Chicago.	" "	"
Baxter, J. F.	Brooklyn.	" "	"
Zimmer, Henry A.	"	Rt. Rev. J. Loughlin.	"
O'Hara, P. F.	"	" "	"
Bartlett, Wm. E.	Baltimore.	His Em. Card. Patrizi.	"
Bloomer, James.	Albany.	Rt. Rev. S. V. Ryan.	"
Hoffmann, John P.	Brooklyn.	" "	"
Dumas, John.	New Orleans.	Mt. Rev. N. J. Perché.	"
Footte, James G.	"	" "	"
Moynahan, Jer.	"	" "	"
Quinlan, William.	Savannah.	Rt. Rev. Ig. Persico.	"
Tuite, Francis.	Hartford.	Rt. Rev. P. A. Pinsonneault	"
Mattingley, Chas. A.	Scranton.	Rt. Rev. Wm. O'Hara.	"
O'Donnell, Hugh R.	Boston.	Mt. Rev. Jas. Bailey.	1873
O'Regan, Bernard.	"	" "	"
Ronan, Michael.	"	" "	"
Stanton, Michael E.	Baltimore.	" "	"
McGuckin, Felix.	Scranton.	" "	"

STUDENTS THAT HAVE BEEN ORDAINED.

NAMES.	DIOCESES.	ORDAINING PRELATES.	YEARS OF ORDINAT.
DASSEL, TH. W.	Scranton.	Rt. Rev. Wm. O'Hara.	1873
CORRIGAN, OWEN B.	Baltimore.	His Em. Card. Patrizi.	"
DOUGHERTY, DAVID.	St. Louis.	" "	"
KLEISER, SOSTH.	"	Rt. Rev. John Henni.	"
POWERS, JOHN.	Hartford.	Rt. Rev. D. W. Bacon.	"
BERONNET, J. M.	New Orleans.	Mt. Rev. N. J. Perché.	"
HOMAN, J. A.	Cincinnati.	Mt. Rev. J. B. Purcell.	"
O'BRIEN, JAMES M.	Savannah.	Rt. Rev. W. H. Gross.	1874
FOWLER, FR. M.	Baltimore.	Mt. Rev. Jas. Bailey.	"
FREDERICK, J. ALPH.	"	" "	"
CUNNINGHAM, JAS. A.	"	" "	"
CURTIS, ALFRED A.[1]	"	" "	"
KEEGAN, STEPHEN.	Boston.	" "	"
KELLY, WILLIAM E.	"	" "	"
GILLIGAN, MICHAEL.	"	" "	"
GLEASON, JAMES J.	Hartford.	" "	"
DONOHOE, JAMES T.	Springfield.	" "	"
HAYES, DENIS.	Chicago.	" "	"
REILLY, JOHN E.	Richmond.	" "	"
DORNEY, MAURICE.	Chicago.	Rt. Rev. T. P. Foley.	"
MACKIN, THOMAS.	"	" "	"
REITMAYER, VIN.	V. A. Colorado.	Rt. Rev. J. P. Machebeuf.	"
GLEESON, M. J.	St. Louis.	Rt. Rev. P. J. Ryan.	"
KIERNAN, OWEN.	Providence.	Rt. Rev. E. C. Fabre.	"
RYAN, WILLIAM H.	Boston.	Rt. Rev. F. McNeirney.	"
DALY, PATRICK V.	Chicago.	Rt. Rev. T. P. Foley.	"
TIERNAN, J. L.	Richmond.	Rt. Rev. Jas. Gibbons.	"
BYRNE, MICHAEL.	Chicago.	Rt. Rev. T. P. Foley.	"
COUGHLAN, ED. L.	Boston.	Mt. Rev. Jas. Bailey.	1875
MURPHY, EDWARD J.	"	" "	"
WALL, JOHN.	"	" "	"
GALLIGAN, MICHAEL.	Hartford.	" "	"
FITZSIMMONS, PETER.	Richmond.	" "	"
DOWLING, D. M.	Chicago.	" "	"
MOORE, PATRICK.	V. A. N. Carolina.	" "	"

[1] The second and present Bishop of Wilmington.

SEMINARY OF ST. SULPICE.

NAMES.	DIOCESES.	ORDAINING PRELATES.	YEARS OF ORDINAT.
McGuire, Patrick.	V. A. Colorado.	Rt. Rev. J. Kain.	1875
Sartori, Joseph A.	Baltimore.	" "	"
Smith, E.	Brooklyn.	Rt. Rev. J. Loughlin.	"
Ward, Thomas.	"	" "	"
McGuire, Peter.	"	Rt. Rev. S. V. Ryan.	"
Murray, Michael F.	"	" "	"
Hurley, Denis.	Josephite.	Rt. Rev. Wm. Weathers.	"
Smith, Ter.	Springfield.	Rt. Rev. P. T. O'Reilly.	"
Reilly, Charles.	Detroit.	Rt. Rev. C. H. Borgess.	"
Gormley, John.	Chicago.	Rt. Rev. T. P. Foley.	"
McShane, Edward.	Buffalo.	Rt. Rev. S. V. Ryan.	"
Daley, Denis.	"	" "	"
Beytagh, Steph. A.	Savannah.	Rt. Rev. Wm. H. Gross.	"
Colbert, Joseph F.	"	" "	"
Sheedy, Patrick.	Boston.	Rt. Rev. E. C. Fabre.	"
Brady, John.	Newark.	Rt. Rev. M. Corrigan.	"
Judge, Charles J.	Baltimore.	His Em. Card. Guibert.	"
Brennan, Mich. J.	"	Rt. Rev. Thos. Becker.	"
Fenne, Matthew A.	"	" "	1876
Patterson, George.	Boston.	" "	"
Lenahan, John F.	Hartford.	" "	"
McCarthy, Jer.	Portland.	Rt. Rev. Jas. A. Healy.	"
Hockeppel, P. W.	Wilmington.	Rt. Rev. Thos. Becker.	"
Tracy, J. A.	Wheeling.	Rt. Rev. J. J. Kain.	"
Dougherty, J. B.	Hartford.	Rt. Rev. S. V. Ryan.	"
Foley, Richard.	Brooklyn.	Rt. Rev. J. Loughlin.	"
McGlinchey, P.	"	" "	"
Hayes, Daniel.	St. Paul.	Rt. Rev. Thos. L. Grace.	"
McCarthy, Eug.	Boston.	Mt. Rev. J. J. Williams.	"
Horgan, Mich. J.	Chicago.	Rt. Rev. T. P. Foley.	"
Powers, John.	"	" "	"
O'Connell, Denis.	Richmond.	His Em. Card. Patrizi.	"
Scholter, Rom.	Green Bay.	Rt. Rev. F. X. Krautbauer.	"
Southgate, Ed. M.	Baltimore.	Mt. Rev. Jas. Gibbons.	1877
Tewes, John F.	"	" "	"
O'Brien, James C.	Hartford.	" "	"
McKenzie, Elias B.	Baltimore.	" "	"

STUDENTS THAT HAVE BEEN ORDAINED. 63

NAMES.	DIOCESES.	ORDAINING PRELATES.	YEARS OF ORDINAT.
TROY, JAMES B.	Boston	Mt. Rev. Jas. Gibbons.	1877
LEE, JAMES.	"	" "	"
McGIVNEY, MICH. J.	Hartford.	" "	"
DENNEHY, JOHN.	Boston.	Mt. Rev. J. J. Williams.	"
PHELAN, MICHAEL.	"	" "	"
MURPHY, J. F. R.	Hartford.	Mt. Rev. Jas. Gibbons.	"
GALLEN, JOSEPH.	Baltimore.	" "	"
DOUGHERTY, CHAS.	Portland.	" "	"
DONAHUE, J. C.	Hartford.	" "	"
MANLEY, D.	Baltimore.	" "	"
PRICE, JOHN C.	Pittsburgh.	Rt. Rev. J. Tuigg.	"
KENNOY, JAMES.	"	" "	"
FISCHER, ANTH.	"	" "	"
MURPHY, JAMES.	Savannah.	Rt. Rev. W. H. Gross.	"
MELONEY, J. P.	St. Louis.	Rt. Rev. R. Seidenbush.	"
McELLIGOTT, JOHN.	Wheeling.	Rt. Rev. J. J. Kain.	"
LECLERC, JOHN M.	V. A. Arizona.	Rt. Rev. J. B. Salpointe.	"
ROUAULT, THEODORE.	"	" "	"
McKEON, MICHAEL.	Hartford.	Rt. Rev. E. C. Fabre.	"
MANNING, PETER.	Baltimore.	Mt. Rev. Jas. Gibbons.	1878
TRUSCHLER, JOS. M.	"	" "	"
McGEE, EDWARD P.	Hartford.	" "	"
WALSH, THADDEUS.	"	" "	"
TREANOR, HUGH.	"	" "	"
CARROLL, J. H.	"	" "	"
McDERMOTT, JOHN F.	Springfield.	" "	"
TARPEY, JOHN LUKE.	"	" "	"
GOGGIN, W. H.	"	" "	"
MEALIA, JAMES F.	Brooklyn.	" "	"
WIGHTMAN, CH. FR.	"	" "	"
O'BRIEN, J. J.	Boston.	" "	"
WHELAN, TIM. JAS.	"	" "	"
COLBERT, JOHN D.	"	" "	"
LYNCH, J. W.	Richmond.	" "	"
NASH, JAMES.	Pittsburgh.	Rt. Rev. J. Tuigg.	"
MALADY, JOHN J.	Pittsburg.	" "	"
RICE, MICHAEL J.	Savannah.	Rt. Rev. W. H. Gross.	"

NAMES.	DIOCESES.	ORDAINING PRELATES.	YEARS OF ORDINAT.
McMahon, Patrick.	Savannah.	Rt. Rev. W. H. Gross.	1878
O'Hara, William.	Peoria.	Rt. Rev. J. L. Spalding.	"
Andries, A.	Natchitoches.	Rt. Rev. F. X. Leray.	"
Ledreux, J. M.	"	" "	"
Dempsey, Ed. J.	St. Louis.	Rt. Rev. P. J. Ryan.	"
Boland, Leo P.	Boston.	Mt. Rev. Dr. Forcade.	"
Doman, Robert F. M.	Detroit.	Rt. Rev. C. H. Borgess.	"
Hund, Francis X.	Covington.	Rt. Rev. A. Toebbe.	"
Broydrick, Thos. J.	Baltimore.	Mt. Rev. Jas. Gibbons.	1879
Boland, John D.	"	" "	"
Dougherty, John J.	"	" "	"
Clarke, Stephen J.	"	" "	"
Montgomery, Geo. T.	San Francisco.	" "	"
Mahoney, Eug. Phil.	Brooklyn.	" "	"
Dunne, Pat'k Wm.	Chicago.	" "	"
Lynch, Michael J.	Hartford.	" "	"
O'Farrell, James T.	Richmond.	" "	"
Gadell, John L.	St. Louis.	" "	"
Drennan, John B.	Springfield.	" "	"
Mariller, J. B. A.	Santa Fé.	Rt. Rev. J. B. Lamy.	"
Shea, Denis A.	Springfield.	Rt. Rev. P. T. O'Reilly.	"
Cunnane, J. A.	Baltimore.	Rt. Rev. Bp. Robert.	"
English, John E.	V.A. Nebraska.	Rt. Rev. S. V. Ryan.	"
Kurz, Bernard.	Brooklyn.	Rt. Rev. J. Loughlin.	"
Waldron, John.	Chicago.	Rt. Rev. Th. P. Foley.	"
McBride, John.	Wheeling.	Rt. Rev. J. J. Kain.	"
McGinley, E. J.	Erie.	Rt. Rev. S. V. Ryan.	"
Maynadier, E. E.	Baltimore.	Rt. Rev. Thos. A. Becker.	1880
Donovan, Jeremiah.	Peoria.	" "	"
Foley, Michael F.	Baltimore.	Mt. Rev. Jas. Gibbons.	"
Leonard, Thomas D.	"	" "	"
Holden, James P.	"	" "	"
Hughes, Thos. B.	"	" "	"
Caughy, N. W.	"	" "	"
Begley, Michael E.	Boston.	" "	"
Galligan, James W.	"	" "	"
O'Donnell, Philip J.	"	" "	"

VERY REV. JOSEPH PAUL DUBREUL,
Fifth Superior of the Seminary.

STUDENTS THAT HAVE BEEN ORDAINED.   65

NAMES.	DIOCESES.	ORDAINING PRELATES.	YEARS OF ORDINAT.
SHANLEY, W. J.	Hartford.	Mt. Rev. Jas. Gibbons.	1880
WINTERS, JOHN THOS.	"	" "	"
GRAGAN, RICH. CH.	"	" "	"
KELLY, EDWARD A.	Chicago.	" "	"
MURRAY, JOHN.	Wheeling.	Rt. Rev. J. J. Kain.	"
MONAGHAN, JOHN J.	Charleston.	Rt. Rev. P. N. Lynch.	"
TUOHY, JOHN T.	St. Louis.	Rt. Rev. W. McCloskey.	"
BRENNAN, MICH. C.	V. A. Colorado.	Rt. Rev. F. McNeirney.	"
LEAVY, PETER.	Detroit.	Rt. Rev. C. H. Borgess.	"
BROCKMANN, FRED.	"	" "	"
FARELLY, PATRICK.	Providence.	Rt. Rev. T. F. Hendricken.	"
MCCABE, PATRICK.	"	" "	"
MCSTEEN, JOHN P.	Pittsburgh.	Rt. Rev. J. Tuigg.	"
GUENDLING, J. H.	Fort Wayne.	Rt. Rev. Jos. Dwenger.	"
CONROY, J. B. H.	La Crosse.	Rt. Rev. M. Heiss.	"
REX, CHARLES B.	Baltimore.	Rt. Rev.T.Cahagne,O.M.C.	"
WAKEHAM, RICH. K.	Richmond.	Mt. Rev. F. B. Richard.	"
JENNINGS, WM. T.	Springfield.	Rt. Rev. P. T. O'Reilly.	"
DYER, E. R.	Baltimore.	Mt. Rev. F. B. Richard.	"
FLANNAGAN, W. E.	Hartford.	Rt. Rev. E. C. Fabre.	"
MCGINTY, JOHN F.	San Francisco.	" "	"
MOYLAN, THOMAS.	Boston.	?	"
O'NEILL, JAMES.	"	?	"
VAN ANTWERP, F. S. J.	Detroit.	Rt. Rev. C. H. Borgess.	"
NORTON, MATTHEW B.	Dubuque.	Rt. Rev. John Hennessy.	"
MELVIN, JAMES.	San Francisco.	Mt. Rev. Jas. Gibbons.	1881
HANAVAN, TER. JOS.	Hartford.	" "	"
CLARKE, EDWARD A.	St. Augustine.	" "	"
PLUNKET, P. H.	Brooklyn.	" "	"
MALADY, DANIEL.	Peoria.	" "	"
KERVICK, THOS. J.	Baltimore.	" "	"
WEIDER, PETER R.	"	" "	"
DONAHUE, JAS. F.	"	" "	"
CASSIDY, JOSEPH H.	"	" "	"
BRÈS, JEROME J.	Natchitoches.	" "	"
O'DONNELL, JAS. H.	Hartford.	" "	"
MULLIGAN, HUGH J.	Boston.	" "	"

SEMINARY OF ST. SULPICE.

NAMES.	DIOCESES.	ORDAINING PRELATES.	YEARS OF ORDINAT.
BILLINGS, PAT'K H.	Boston.	Mt. Rev. Jas. Gibbons.	1881
SEXTON, PHIL. FR.	"	" "	"
BYRNES, EDWARD P.	"	" "	"
BOYLE, PATRICK J.	V. A. Nebraska.	" "	"
MURRAY, B. P.	Chicago.	" "	"
HART, WILLIAM H.	Springfield.	" "	"
PITAVAL, J. B.	V. A. Colorado.	Rt. Rev. J. P. Machebeuf.	"
SERVANT, ROBERT.	"	" "	"
SINGLETON, JOHN J.	Cincinnati.	Rt. Rev. W. H. Elder.	"
GOULET, AMBROSE J.	Chicago.	Mt. Rev. P. A. Feehan.	"
BAART, PETER A.	Detroit.	Rt. Rev. C. H. Borgess.	"
REYNOLDS, THOS.	Springfield.	Rt. Rev. P. T. O'Reilly.	"
WALL, JULIAN.	Boston.	Mt. Rev. Jas. Gibbons.	1882
FITZGERALD, JOS. A.	"	" "	"
KELLY, MARTIN.	"	" "	"
KELLY, JAMES F.	"	" "	"
HISHEN, DENIS.	Chicago.	" "	"
KELLY, OWEN.	"	" "	"
MEEHAN, LAURENCE.	"	" "	"
DUNNE, J. M.	"	" "	"
FITZSIMMONS, MICH. J.	"	Mt. Rev. P. A. Feehan.	"
LONERGAN, ARTH. F.	"	" "	"
QUINN, J. J.	Peoria.	Mt. Rev. Jas. Gibbons.	"
KANE, PATRICK J.	St. Louis.	" "	"
NUGENT, FR. J.	V. A. Nebraska.	" "	"
HANNAN, JAMES S.	"	" "	"
THOMAS, CORN. F.	Baltimore.	" "	"
DUNN, J. E.	"	" "	"
WUNDER, EDWARD J.	"	" "	"
BRENNAN, MICH. J.	"	" "	"
MCGINITY, EDWARD.	V. A. N. Carolina.	" "	"
FRIOLI, JOSEPH.	Richmond.	" "	"
MERRIEN, PIERRE Y.	V. A. Arizona.	" "	"
CASSIDY, MICHAEL P.	Providence.	" "	"
O'BRIEN, GEORGE.	Savannah.	Rt. Rev. W. H. Gross.	"
MCCARTHY, WM. A.	"	" "	"
DOTTMAN, BERNARD.	Cincinnati.	Mt. Rev. W. H. Elder.	"

STUDENTS THAT HAVE BEEN ORDAINED. 67

NAMES.	DIOCESES.	ORDAINING PRELATES.	YEARS OF ORDINAT.
KLOSTERMAN, JOS.	Cincinnati.	Mt. Rev. W. H. Elder.	1882
KILCOYNE, ANT. J. F.	St. Augustine.	Rt. Rev. J. J. Tuigg.	"
GOURCY, JOSEPH.	Santa Fé.	Mt. Rev. J. B. Lamy.	"
MANLEY, MICHAEL J.	V. A. N. Carolina.	Rt. Rev. S. V. Ryan.	"
GARNIER, J. M.	Santa Fé.	Mt. Rev. J. B. Lamy.	"
CONNELLY, J. M.	Baltimore.	H. E. Card. M. La Valetta.	"
CONSIDINE, WM.	Detroit.	Rt. Rev. C. H. Borgess.	"
KELEHER, DAN. J.	Boston.	Mt. Rev. Jas. Gibbons.	1883
NEVES, A. G. DA S.	Providence.	" "	"
O'BRIEN, TIM. M.	Hartford.	" "	"
DONAHOE, JOHN F.	Albany.	" "	"
RIGNEY, MICHAEL F.	Hartford.	" "	"
MARR, JAMES DON.	Baltimore	Rt. Rev. J. J. Keane.	"
GREENE, JOHN J.	Chicago.	" "	"
O'REILLY, EDWARD.	"	" "	"
LAWLER, JOSEPH.	Trenton.	" "	"
DONOHOE, CHAS. E.	Richmond.	" "	"
DEGNAN, JAMES P.	Hartford.	" "	"
DOUGHERTY, WM. T.	Providence.	" "	"
MOORE, BEN. F.	Peoria.	" "	"
GILFETHER, JAS. F.	Boston.	" "	"
DOODY, MICHAEL J.	"	" "	"
CROWLEY, DENIS O.	San Francisco.	" "	"
HOCTOR, ISAAC J.	Cincinnati.	Mt. Rev. W. H. Elder.	"
CONWAY, WILLIAM.	"	" "	"
HICKEY, E. P.	"	" "	"
CRUMLEY, JAMES.	Grand Rapids.	Rt. Rev. H. J. Richter.	"
LANDERS, JAMES.	Detroit.	Rt. Rev. C. H. Borgess.	"
CROWE, JOHN A.	Boston.	Rt. Rev. P. T. O'Reilly.	"
MCAVOY, JAMES H.	"	" "	"
O'KEEFE, THOS.	Springfield.	" "	"
FOLEY, JEREMIAH.	St. Louis.	Rt. Rev. P. J. Ryan.	"
CURTIN, JEREMIAH.	Hartford.	Rt. Rev. L. McMahon.	"
WERNINGER, JOS. W.	Wheeling.	Rt. Rev. J. J. Kain.	"
RUDOLPH, CHRIST.	Philadelphia.	?	"
SMITH, WILLIAM J.	S. P. M.	Rt Rev. J. Loughlin.	"
LENEGHAN, P. H.	Baltimore.	Mt. Rev. Jas Gibbons.	"

SEMINARY OF ST. SULPICE.

NAMES.	DIOCESES.	ORDAINING PRELATES.	YEARS OF ORDINAT.
Darcy, J. J.	Chicago.	Mt. Rev. P. A. Feehan.	1883
Quinn, John P.	Peoria.	Rt. Rev. J. L. Spalding.	"
Carey, John J.	Detroit.	Rt. Rev. C. H. Borgess.	"
McDermott, J. J.	Baltimore.	Mt. Rev. Jas. Gibbons.	"
Massardier, J. M.	New Orleans.	Mt. Rev. F. X. Leray.	"
Kinsella, Ger. A.	Chicago.	Mt. Rev. P. A. Feehan.	"
Fallon, John J.	Springfield.	Rt. Rev. P. T. O'Reilly.	"
Goupeaud, John.	Brooklyn.	Rt. Rev. J. Loughlin.	"
Donovan, William.	Trenton.	Rt. Rev. M. J. O'Farrell.	"
Haygh, Joseph.	Baltimore.	Rt. Rev. Dr. Fleck.	"
Dower, William J.	Springfield.	Rt. Rev. P. T. O'Reilly.	"
Rosensteel, Chas. O.	Baltimore.	Mt. Rev. Jas. Gibbons.	1884
Mercer, Thomas J.	Richmond.	" "	"
Tabb, John B.	"	" "	"
Courtney, Mich. J.	Springfield.	" "	"
Harmon, John F.	"	" "	"
Mahoney, James F.	Davenport.	" "	"
Sheehan, Maurice J.	Hartford.	" "	"
O'Keefe, John D.	Providence.	" "	"
Kelly, Thomas L.	"	" "	"
Murphy, Denis E.	"	" "	"
Malone, Thomas H.	Peoria.	Rt. Rev. D. M. Bradley.	"
Tierney, Matthew J.	Brooklyn.	Rt. Rev. J. Loughlin.	"
Fitzgerald, John G.	"	" "	"
O'Dougherty, C. H.	"	" "	"
O'Reilly, M. A.	Trenton.	" "	"
McGowan, Chas. J.	Hartford.	Rt. Rev. L. McMahon.	"
Sullivan, John W.	Boston.	Mt. Rev. J. J. Williams.	"
Greene, Joseph P.	Chicago.	Mt. Rev. P. A. Feehan.	"
Sullivan, Laur. M.	Cincinnati.	Mt. Rev. W. H. Elder.	"
Buckley, Daniel A.	"	" "	"
McCormick, Wm.	Davenport.	Rt. Rev. H. Cosgrove.	"
Meathe, Matthew.	Detroit.	Rt. Rev. C. H. Borgess.	"
Mulgrew, Jas. Thos.	Peoria.	Rt. Rev. T. F. Hendricken.	"
Coroner, J. J.	Scranton.	Rt. Rev. W. O'Hara.	"
Harmon, John F.	Springfield.	Rt. Rev. P. T. O'Reilly.	"
McNulty, Miles H.	Lacrosse.	Mt. Rev. M. Heiss.	"

STUDENTS THAT HAVE BEEN ORDAINED.

NAMES.	DIOCESES.	ORDAINING PRELATES.	YEARS OF ORDINAT.
KROLL, F. X.	Detroit.	Rt. Rev. C. H. Borgess.	1884
CARR, ANDREW.	Chicago.	Mt. Rev. P. A. Feehan.	"
WHALEN, THOMAS L.	Grand Rapids.	Rt. Rev. H. J. Richter.	"
COOK, JOHN A.	Davenport.	Rt. Rev. T. A. Becker.	"
FLANAGAN, J. T.	Davenport.	Rt. Rev. H. Cosgrove.	1885
REILLY, THOMAS J.	Columbus.	Rt. Rev. J. B. Brondel.	"
SLATTERY, LAUR. W.	Boston.	Mt. Rev. Jas. Gibbons.	"
WELCH, MICH. JAS.	"	" "	"
ROWAN, PATRICK H.	Vincennes.	" "	"
ALTHOFF, AUGUST.	Natchez.	" "	"
DONAHUE, PAT'K J.	Baltimore.	" "	"
REARDON, WM. A.	"	" "	"
GWYNN, EUGENE S.	"	" "	"
WHELAN, JOHN T.	"	" "	"
HANNAN, EUGENE A.	"	" "	"
DINNEEN, MICHAEL J.	Richmond.	" "	"
BOWLER, JOHN J.	"	" "	"
DRAKE, RICHARD A.	"	" "	"
MOORE, JOHN J.	Boston.	" "	"
SCANLAN, MART. P.	San Francisco.	" "	"
FITZGERALD, ED. ST.	Springfield.	" "	"
CARROLL, STEPHEN F.	Omaha.	" "	"
HOLTHAUS, JOHN H.	Cincinnati.	Mt. Rev. W. H. Elder.	"
CUSACK, JOHN.	"	" "	"
SOURD, ADOL. F.	"	" "	"
GALLEN, JOSEPH A.	Harrisburg.	Rt. Rev. J. J. Keane.	"
PERRY, FRANK N.	Chicago.	Mt. Rev. P. A. Feehan.	"
HITCHCOCK, JOHN N.	"	" "	"
KEARNS, THOMAS A.	"	" "	"
FAGAN, EDWARD J.	Boston.	Mt. Rev. J. J. Williams.	"
KELLY, HUGH B.	Davenport.	" "	"
McGRONEN, THOS. F.	Brooklyn.	Rt. Rev. J. Loughlin.	"
CURLEY, W. H.	Providence.	Rt. Rev. T. F. Hendricken.	"
TIGHE, THOMAS.	Springfield.	Rt. Rev. P. T. O'Reilly.	"
ANDRÉ, LOUIS.	Santa Fé.	Mt. Rev. J. B. Salpointe.	"
McKENNA, PETER.	Providence.	Mt. Rev. E. C. Fabre.	"
HANRAHAN, THOS. S.	Springfield.	Rt. Rev. P. T. O'Reilly.	"

NAMES.	DIOCESES.	ORDAINING PRELATES.	YEARS OF ORDINAT.
HEALEY, TIMOTHY J.	St. Paul.	Rt. Rev. S. V. Ryan.	1885
HUMMERT, J. B.	Davenport.	Mt. Rev. P. A. Feehan.	"
RYAN, THOMAS J.	Detroit.	Rt. Rev. C. H. Borgess.	"
GARRY, JAMES.	"	" "	"
FALLON, E. J.	New Orleans.	Mt. Rev. F. X. Leray.	"
BAUER, J.	Grand Rapids.	Rt. Rev. J. H. Richter.	"
FITZGERALD, ROB. J.	St. Paul.	Rt. Rev. S. V. Ryan.	"
DARCHE, LIG.	San Antonio.	Rt. Rev. J. C. Neraz.	"
STAPLETON, THOS. E.	Baltimore.	Mt. Rev. Jas. Gibbons.	1886
HAECKLER, JOHN B.	Pittsburg.	" "	"
McDONALD, ROBERT.	"	" "	"
FREEMAN, JAS. CHR.	Omaha.	" "	"
DOLPHIN, JOHN F.	St. Paul.	" "	"
SCHMITT, JOSEPH.	Columbus.	His Em. Card. Gibbons.	"
NIEWENHAUS, H. A. M.	New York.	" "	"
McCUE, JOHN J.	San Francisco.	" "	"
CAHALAN, JOHN J.	Columbus.	" "	"
WILLIAMS, ED. AUG.	Baltimore.	" "	"
McGEE, JOSEPH F.	"	" "	"
GRIFFITH, PAUL.	"	" "	"
BART, CHARLES M.	"	" "	"
MATTHEWS, JAMES R.	"	" "	"
MANLEY, JOHN B.	"	" "	"
MURPHY, MICHAEL F.	Boston.	" "	"
LUCKE, FREDERICK J.	Richmond.	Rt. Rev. J. J. Keane.	"
PAYNE, WILLIAM G.	"	Mt. Rev. Abp. Lenti.	"
KOENIG, HENRY C.	Detroit.	Mt. Rev. M. Heiss.	"
CAHILL, THOMAS.	Brooklyn.	Rt. Rev. J. Loughlin.	"
BRANCHEAU, L. I.	Detroit.	Rt. Rev. C. H. Borgess.	"
PRICE, T. FREDERICK.	V. A. N. Carolina.	Rt. Rev. H. P. Northrop.	"
KEARNEY, THOMAS.	Chicago.	Mt. Rev. P. A. Feehan.	"
MULDOON, PETER J.	"	Rt. Rev. J. Loughlin.	"
SCHREIBER, JOHN M.	Detroit.	Rt. Rev. C. H. Borgess.	"
FLEMING, MICHAEL J.	"	" "	"
O'CONNOR, P. J.	Chicago.	Mt. Rev. P. A. Feehan.	"
WEITEKAMP, H. F.	Brooklyn.	Rt. Rev. J. Loughlin.	"
HICKEY, CHARLES A.	Cincinnati.	Mt. Rev. W. H. Elder.	"

His Eminence James Cardinal Gibbons,
Archbishop of Baltimore.

STUDENTS THAT HAVE BEEN ORDAINED.

NAMES.	DIOCESES.	ORDAINING PRELATES.	YEARS OF ORDINAT.
VON DER AHE, G. N.	Cincinnati.	Mt. Rev. W. H. Elder.	1886
GERDES, ALOYSIUS.	"	" "	"
NEVILLE, M. P.	"	" "	"
KELLY, NICHOLAS J.	"	" "	"
MCCAUGHAN, W. C.	Springfield.	Rt. Rev. P. T. O'Reilly.	"
CRUSE, J. M.	"	" "	"
FOLEY, MICHAEL F.	Pittsburgh.	Rt. Rev. R. Phelan.	"
NACEY, ALONZO H. B.	Detroit.	Rt. Rev. C. H. Borgess.	"
GOLDRICK, L. P.	"	" "	"
O'RORKE, T. F.	"	" "	"
DUFFY, E. A. L.	Brooklyn.	Mt. Rev. F. B. Richard.	"
LA BRIE, ARMAND.	Chicago.	Mt. Rev. P. A. Feehan.	"
FITZGERALD, J. J.	Louisville.	Rt. Rev. W. McCloskey.	"
DOYLE, JAMES H.	Springfield.	Rt. Rev. P. Machebeuf.	"
BYRNE, JOHN F.	Ogdensburg.	Rt. Rev. E. Wadhams.	"
REINHARDT, NICH.	New York.	Rt. Rev. B. McQuaid.	"
DWYER, PATRICK C.	St. Paul.	Rt. Rev. J. Ireland.	"
SOUMIS, JOSEPH.	"	" "	"
GIBBONS, J. J.	Denver.	Mt. Rev. P. A. Feehan.	"
RYAN, W. B.	Covington.	Rt. Rev. P. C. Maes.	"
MCSORLEY, JOSEPH.	Charleston.	Rt. Rev. H. P. Northrop.	"
DALEY, JOHN P.	Mobile.	Rt. Rev. A. A. Curtis.	1887
O'HARA, WILLIAM L.	Brooklyn.	" "	"
MAHONEY, TIM. J.	Boston.	Rt. Rev. Matth. Harkins.	"
ROCHE, THOS. ALPH.	Trenton.	His Em. Card. Gibbons.	"
CONNELLY, FR. J. P.	Wilmington.	" "	"
MCKINNON, WM. D.	San Francisco.	" "	"
BROWN, GEORGE.	" "	" "	"
GLAAB, GEORGE.	Baltimore.	" "	"
DILLON, JOHN J.	"	" "	"
O'CONNELL, PAT'K J.	"	" "	"
KENNEDY, ROB. FR.	Savannah.	" "	"
HOLLERAN, STEPHEN.	Louisville.	" "	"
KENNEDY, THOMAS F.	Providence.	" "	"
MILLER, WILLIAM H.	Trenton.	" "	"
GEOGHEGAN, DAN. P.	"	" "	"
KAYLOR, GEO. WM.	Pittsburgh.	" "	"

SEMINARY OF ST. SULPICE.

NAMES.	DIOCESES.	ORDAINING PRELATES.	YEARS OF ORDINAT.
Downey, John J.	Hartford.	His Em. Card. Gibbons.	1887
Fallon, Theodore P.	San Francisco.	" "	"
Doran, Edward J.	" "	" "	"
O'Neile, Charles E.	" "	" "	"
Yorke, Pet. Christ.	" "	" "	"
Campbell, Fred. W.	Wilmington.	" "	"
O'Grady, Henry.	Mobile.	" "	"
Rempe, Joseph.	Chicago.	Mt. Rev. P. A. Feehan.	"
Jennings, James J.	"	" "	"
Burke, Patrick.	Springfield.	Rt. Rev. P. T. O'Reilly.	"
Shee, Joseph.	Cincinnati.	His Em. Card. Parocchi.	"
O'Brien, Matth. P.	"	Mt. Rev. W. H. Elder.	"
Moeller, Bernard.	"	" "	"
Proepperman, Hy.	"	" "	"
Ryan, John P.	Detroit.	Rt. Rev. C. H. Borgess.	"
Ternes, Anthony P.	"	" "	"
Sadlier, Richard.	"	" "	"
Hennessy, Thomas G.	"	" "	"
Kramer, J. F.	"	" "	"
Gore, J. J.	"	" "	"
Granger, Joseph M.	Galveston.	Rt. Rev. N. A. Gallagher.	"
Moise, R. V.	New Orleans.	Mt. Rev. F. X. Leray.	"
Alonzo, Nicom.	Mexico.	Mt. Rev. Dr. Labastida.	"
Schwalen, Bern.	Covington.	Rt. Rev. P. C. Maes.	"
Meade, John.	Columbus.	" "	"
Heaney, James.	Peoria.	Rt. Rev. S. V. Ryan.	"
McLaughlin, Philip.	Harrisburg.	" "	"
Allen, James.	San Francisco.	Mt. Rev. P. W. Riordan.	"
Dumas, Regis.	Natchitoches.	Rt. Rev. A. Durier.	"
Rechatin, J. J.	"	" "	"
Arnaud, C.	"	" "	"
Piegay, Anthony.	"	" "	"
Rivallier, Fr.	Denver.	Rt. Rev. N. Matz.	"
Szmigiel, Alex.	Pittsburg.	Rt. Rev. R. Phelan.	"
Kirner, Thomas J.	"	" "	"
Sheehy, J. E.	S. P. M.	Rt. Rev. M. O'Farrell.	"
Schulze, John H.	Leavenworth.	Rt. Rev. L. M. Fink.	"

STUDENTS THAT HAVE BEEN ORDAINED. 73

NAMES.	DIOCESES.	ORDAINING PRELATES.	YEARS OF ORDINAT.
PIMENTEL, JOAQ. JOS.	San Francisco.	His Em. Card. Gibbons.	1888
SHIELDS, JOSEPH F.	St. Louis.	" "	"
REANEY, WM. H. I.	Baltimore.	" "	"
YORK, THOMAS A.	Louisville.	" "	"
DALY, JOHN A.	Wilmington.	" "	"
WALSH, SIMON B.	Trenton.	" "	"
LIMAGNE, JOHN B.	Natchitoches.	" "	"
FALLON, WILLIAM A.	Richmond.	" "	"
McCANN, J. J.	Chicago.	" "	"
SCANLAN, MICHAEL.	San Francisco.	" "	"
MULLIGAN, PAT'K E.	" "	" "	"
CULLEN, ARTHUR H.	Westminster (Eng.).	" "	"
OPYRCHALSKI, LEOP.	Grand Rapids.	Rt. Rev. H. J. Richter.	"
WARLUZEL, ALB. H.	V. A. Arizona.	Rt. Rev. C. H. Borgess.	"
FLETCHER, WM. A.	Baltimore.	His Em. Card. Gibbons.	"
DOORY, FR. P.	"	" "	"
LYONS, THOMAS E.	"	" "	"
O'BRIEN, JOSEPH TH.	"	" "	"
ELBERT, CASPAR P.	"	" "	"
McCABE, DENIS.	Vincennes.	" "	"
TAVARES, JOHN M.	San Francisco.	" "	"
NEALON, THOS. ALOY.	Hartford.	" "	"
LEININGER, ARTH. L.	Columbus.	" "	"
CAREY, MICHAEL H.	Brooklyn.	Rt. Rev. J. Loughlin.	"
BELFORD, JOHN L.	"	" "	"
KIRBY, WILLIAM J.	"	" "	"
FLAHERTY, MICH. J.	"	" "	"
DOTZAUER, FRED.WM.	"	" "	"
REYNOLDS, FR. L.	Chicago.	Mt. Rev. P. A. Feehan.	"
PICKHAM, DANIEL J.	"	" "	"
McGAVICK, JAMES.	"	" "	"
O'CALLAGHAN, MICH.	Peoria.	" "	"
FLOOD, BERNARD.	Davenport.	" "	"
VOGT, J. J.	Pittsburg.	Rt. Rev. R. Phelan.	"
LUDDEN, JOHN J.	"	" "	"
FERGUSSON, JAMES P.	San Francisco.	Mt. Rev. P. W. Riordan.	"
NAUROCKI, ST.	Chicago.	Mt. Rev. P. A. Feehan.	"
LANGE, J.	"	" "	"

NAMES.	DIOCESES.	ORDAINING PRELATES.	YEARS OF ORDINAT.
McKinnery, Thomas.	Peoria.	Rt. Rev. J. L. Spalding.	1888
Murtagh, William.	"	" "	"
Barry, John.	"	" "	"
Tragesser, George.	Baltimore.	Mt. Rev. Dr. Laouenan.	"
McKenny, Fr. X.	"	Mt. Rev. F. B. Richard.	"
Dacey, John.	Oblate of Mary.	Mt. Rev. J. J. Williams.	"
Kunes, Joseph.	Marquette.	Rt. Rev. J. Vertin.	"
Fagan, James P.	Scranton.	Rt. Rev. W. O'Hara.	"
O'Reilly, James A.	"	" "	"
Colligan, P. J.	"	" "	"
Hussey, James.	"	" "	"
Rufe, August H.	Philadelphia.	Mt. Rev. P. W. Riordan.	"
Mugan, Charles.	Omaha.	Mt. Rev. P. A. Feehan.	"
Loughran, J. J.	Lincoln.	Mt. Rev. J. J. Lynch.	"
Hayden, Lawrence.	Havre de Grace, N. F.	Rt. Rev. R. MacDonald.	"
Walsh, Thomas J.	Cincinnati.	Mt. Rev. W. H. Elder.	"
Hoffmann, Peter.	Davenport.	Rt. Rev. H. Cosgrove.	"
Cluney, Martin.	Rochester.	Rt. Rev. B. McQuaid.	"
Ternes, P. J.	Detroit.	Rt. Rev. C. H. Borgess.	"
McLaughlin, Dan.	"	" "	"
Neale, John.	Hartford.	Mt. Rev. J. J. Williams.	"
Liebana, Mag.	Los Angeles.	Rt. Rev. F. Mora.	"
Beutgen, Peter.	Oregon.	Mt. Rev. W. H. Gross.	"
Noel, Fabian.	"	" "	"
Byrne, M. J.	Fort Wayne.	Rt. Rev. J. Dwenger.	"
McKechnie, J. H.	Springfield.	Rt. Rev. P. T. O'Reilly.	"
Feys, Jerome.	Covington.	Rt. Rev. P. C. Maes.	"
Mestress, Ramon M.	Los Angeles.	Rt. Rev. F. Mora.	"
Brannan, P. F.	Galveston.	Rt. Rev. N. A. Gallagher.	"
Riordan, Mich. J.	Baltimore.	His Em. Card. Parocchi.	"
Darche, Joseph J.	S. P. M.	Rt. Rev. J. Loughlin.	"
Russell, Wm. Thos.	"	His Em. Card. Gibbons.	1889
Weigand, Joseph A.	Columbus.	" "	"
Crean, Richard A.	Trenton.	" "	"
Early, Robert.	Hartford.	" "	"
Ferrer, Raymond.	Josephite.	" "	"
Heffernan, Mich. P.	"	" "	"

STUDENTS THAT HAVE BEEN ORDAINED.

NAMES.	DIOCESES.	ORDAINING PRELATES.	YEARS OF ORDINAT.
GALLAGHER, THOS. E.	Baltimore.	His Em. Card. Gibbons.	1889
CAMPBELL, RICH. C.	"	" "	"
O'NEILL, RICHARD.	"	" "	"
LUCAS, GEORGE J.	Scranton.	" "	"
QUIRK, JOHN WM.	Providence.	" "	"
BENNETT, JOS. ALPH.	Brooklyn.	" "	"
GRADY, HENRY TH.	Boston.	" "	"
O'REILLY, ARTHUR J.	St. Louis.	Mt. Rev. P. R. Kenrick.	"
MICKLE, EDWARD.	Wilmington.	His Em. Card. Parocchi.	"
DOLAN, E. J.	Boston.	Mt. Rev. J. J. Williams.	"
HANNAWIN, F. P.	"	" "	"
LEMKE, JOHN.	Detroit.	Rt. Rev. J. S. Foley.	"
DENNISON, JOHN.	Chicago.	Mt. Rev. P. A. Feehan.	"
O'REILLY, JOSEPH P.	Chicago.	Mt. Rev. P. A. Feehan.	"
WHALEN, THOMAS J.	"	" "	"
MANIETT, HENRY.	Davenport.	Rt. Rev. H. Cosgrove.	"
DONOVAN, JAS.	Pittsburg.	Rt. Rev. R. Phelan.	"
McGINLEY, JOHN P.	Brooklyn.	Rt. Rev. J. Loughlin.	"
STANTON, J. F.	Vincennes.	Rt. Rev. F. S. Chatard.	"
JORDAN, JAMES P.	Scranton.	Rt. Rev. W. O'Hara.	"
SMYTH, NICHOLAS.	"	" "	"
O'DONNELL, WM.	"	" "	"
WINTERS, PETER.	"	" "	"
GIRIMONDI, JOHN B.	"	" "	"
HALLEY, JOSEPH.	Detroit.	Rt. Rev. J. S. Foley.	"
KENNEDY, THOS. F.	"	" "	"
CHODNIEWICZ, F.	"	" "	"
LAMPING, FR.	Cincinnati.	Mt. Rev. W. H. Elder.	"
MULVIHILLE, MICH.	"	" "	"
NODLER, ALBERT.	Davenport.	His Em. Card. Parocchi.	"
HENNESSY, PATK. F.	Louisville.	Rt. Rev. Wm. McCloskey.	"
CORBETT, MARTIN.	Lincoln.	Rt. Rev. Th. Bonacum.	"
McCANN, CHRIST.	Hartford.	Rt. Rev. L. McMahon.	"
HOVORA, FR. X.	Lincoln.	Rt. Rev. Th. Bonacum.	"
TREANOR, JAMES J.	St. Paul.	Mt. Rev. J. Ireland.	"
LYONS, PATRICK.	Springfield.	Rt. Rev. N. Matz.	"
McCAUGHEN, JOHN P.	"	Rt. Rev. P. T. O'Reilly.	"

76   SEMINARY OF ST. SULPICE.

NAMES.	DIOCESES.	ORDAINING PRELATES.	YEARS OF ORDINAT.
IVERS, JOHN C.	Springfield.	Rt. Rev. P. T. O'Reilly.	1889
CUNNINGHAM, E. A.	Hobart (Tasmania).	Rt. Rev. D. Murphy.	"
CHALOUPKA, STANIS.	Springfield.	Rt. Rev. P. T. O'Reilly.	"
MURRAY, JOHN J.	Baltimore.	His Em. Card. Gibbons.	1890
HANEKE, AUGUST B.	"	"	"
MONTEVERDE, T. J.	"	"	"
KANE, WILLIAM J.	"	"	"
MORAN, MATTHEW.	"	"	"
FITZGERALD, JAS. P.	"	"	"
CRIMMINS, DAVID.	Chicago.	"	"
MCCARRON, J. J.	Brooklyn.	"	"
OTT, GEORGE L.	Wilmington.	"	"
CONLEY, JAMES H.	Lincoln.	"	"
EHRHART, ERNEST.	New Orleans.	"	"
BLANC, AUGUSTUS.	"	"	"
KENNY, THOMAS J.	Baltimore.	"	"
NOLAN, JAMES F.	"	"	"
STANTON, THOS. J.	"	"	"
MEALEY, E. J.	Wilmington.	"	"
QUIGLEY, JAMES P.	"	Mt. Rev. J. J. Williams.	"
KNIERY, EDWARD J.	Peoria.	Rt. Rev. J. L. Spalding.	"
GOECKEL, CHARLES J.	Scranton.	Rt. Rev. Wm. O'Hara.	"
FINN, THOMAS.	Chicago.	Mt. Rev. P. A. Feehan.	"
MELODY, JOHN.	"	"	"
VAN PELT, HENRY.	"	"	"
BOHAL, THOMAS.	"	"	"
MATTINGLEY, J. B.	Columbus.	Rt. Rev. J. A. Watterson.	"
TEAHAN, JAS. F. X.	Springfield.	Rt. Rev. P. T. O'Reilly.	"
CUSACK, JAMES T.	Covington.	Rt. Rev. P. C. Maes.	"
MAHER, DANIEL.	Pittsburg.	His Em. Card. Richard.	"
HOAG, CHARLES D.	Baltimore.	Mt. Rev. Wm. Walsh.	"
O'KANE, ROBERT E.	Wheeling.	Rt. Rev. J. J. Kain.	"
GALLIGAN, CHARLES.	Harrisburg.	Rt. Rev. A. A. Curtis.	"
BACCIOCHI, ALFRED.	New Orleans.	Mt. Rev. F. Janssens.	"
BULOT, A. P.	"	"	"
BAUDRILLARD, P.	V. A. Arizona.	Rt. Rev. P. Bourgade.	"
DESMARAIS, LOUIS.	Oregon.	Mt. Rev. E. C. Fabre.	"

VERY REV. A. L. MAGNIEN, D. D.,
Superior of the Seminary.

STUDENTS THAT HAVE BEEN ORDAINED.

NAMES.	DIOCESES.	ORDAINING PRELATES.	YEARS OF ORDINAT.
PYNE, MICHAEL.	Buffalo.	Rt. Rev. Wm. O'Hara.	1890
AHMAN, IGNATIUS.	Covington.	His Em. Card. Parocchi.	"
CAHILL, CHAS. H. B.	Cincinnati.	Mt. Rev. W. H. Elder.	"
MOORE, JAMES A.	"	" "	"
FRANZ, JOHN G.	"	" "	"
MULCAHY, DENIS O.	Detroit.	Rt. Rev. J. S. Foley.	"
CLERMONT, LOUIS.	Burlington.	Rt. Rev. L. de Goesbriand.	"
MORRISSEY, J. J.	Chicago.	Mt. Rev. P. A. Feehan.	"
LONEY, MICHAEL G.	Cincinnati.	Mt. Rev. W. H. Elder.	"
McKINNON, BERN. J.	San Francisco.	His Em. Card. Gibbons.	1891
PHELAN, CORN. FR.	Trenton.	" "	"
ILLIG, JOSEPH AL.	St. Paul.	" "	"
HEALY, JOHN.	Chicago.	Mt. Rev. P. A. Feehan.	"
GLENNEN, JOSEPH A.	"	" "	"
SWANSON, F. B.	"	" "	"
BYRNE, P. F.	"	Mt. Rev. J. J. Williams.	"
GARDNER, WILLIAM.	Brooklyn.	Rt. Rev. J. J. Loughlin.	"
CROWLEY, DENIS J.	Wilmington.	Mt. Rev. J. J. Williams.	"
GOREY, JAMES L.	Covington.	Rt. Rev. P. C. Maes.	"
BYRNE, CHRIST. S.	St. Louis.	Mt. Rev. P. R. Kenrick.	"
DUNPHY, WILLIAM F.	Trenton.	Rt. Rev. M. O'Farrell.	"
MAURER, GEORGE J.	Detroit.	Rt. Rev. J. S. Foley.	"
MULLER, F. A.	"	" "	"
COLGAN, E. J.	Providence.	Rt. Rev. M. Harkins.	"
SULLIVAN, J. F.	"	" "	"
KELLY, J. S.	Peoria.	Rt. Rev. Jas. Ryan.	"
TOBIN, THOMAS V.	Nashville.	Rt. Rev. J. Rademacher.	"
McCABE, H. R.	Detroit.	Rt. Rev. J. Vertin.	"
DOUGHERTY, GEO. A.	Baltimore.	His Em. Card. Parocchi.	"
WALSH, THOMAS.	St. Louis.	" "	"
DUFFY, DANIEL.	Baltimore.	Rt. Rev. I. M. Potron, M.O.	"
McSHANE, PATRICK S.	Lincoln.	Rt. Rev. Thos. Bonacum.	"
WOLFGARTEN, ANT. J.	Chicago.	Mt. Rev. F. X. Katzer.	"
SPERLEIN, FRED.	Marquette.	Mt. Rev. E. C. Fabre.	"
DUNNE, DANIEL A.	Scranton.	Rt. Rev. R. Phelan.	"
CLANCY, JOHN J.	Alton.	Rt. Rev. James Ryan.	"
REILLY, J. H.	Louisville.	Rt. Rev. Wm. McCloskey.	"

STUDENTS OF ST. MARY'S COLLEGE.

The Seminary will be under obligations to any reader sending notice of inaccuracies or omissions in the following lists.

NAME.	RESIDENCE.	ENTRY AND DEPARTURE.
GUTTIEREZ, PEDRO.	Havana.	1799—1800
AZCARATTE, JOSEPH.	"	" —1803
RUITZ, NICHOLAS.	"	" — "
DUBOURG, ARNAULD.	San Domingo.	" — ?
PAGOT, JOSEPH.	" "	" —1800
LA REINTRIE, J. B.	" "	" —1803
MEYNADIER, FREDERICK.	" "	" —1800
LE BATARD, GERMAIN.	" "	" — ?
COTTINEAU, DENIS.	" "	" —1803
COTTINEAU, ACHILLE.	" "	" —1802
DE MUN, N. AMÉDÉE, A. B.	" "	" —1806
BASILE, JEAN.	" "	" —1800
PLUNKETT, EDWARD.	" "	" —1801
DARNAUD, AMÉDÉE.	" "	" —1802
FLÉCHIER, EUGÈNE.	" "	" —1801
CARLE, PAULE.	Jamaica.	" —1805
DE ST. CASTOR, H.	"	1800—1801
DE ST. CASTOR, J.	"	" — "
PETIT, LOUIS.	"	" —1803
COMTE, CECIL.	San Domingo.	" — "
COMTE, JULES.	" "	" — "
SENAT, GEORGE.	New York.	" —1804
SENAT, PROSPER.	" "	" — "
LORQUET, HENRY.	San Domingo.	" —1801
PASCAULT, LOUIS.	Baltimore.	" —1802
XAUPI, HONORÉ.	San Domingo.	" —1801
SENAT, JOHN.	New York.	" —1804

NAME.	RESIDENCE.	ENTRY AND DEPARTURE.
WALSH, ROBERT, A. M.	Baltimore.	1800—1801
DEL CASTILLO, JOSEPH.	Havana.	" — ?
DESMANGLES, ELOY.	San Domingo.	1801— ?
MAURAU, J. B., A. M.	" "	" —1806
VIGURI, RAYMOND.	Havana.	" —1803
LE MEILLEUR, RÉNÉ.	San Domingo.	" — "
MONTALVO, JOSEPH M.	Havana.	" — "
MONTALVO, LORENZO.	"	" — "
RATTIER, N.	New York.	" —1802
TOUSON.	San Domingo.	" —1805
FIGUERRA, L.	Havana.	" —1803
FIGUERRA, ANTONIO.	"	" — "
RUIZ DE LA PEÑA, A.	"	1801—1803
RICHER, A.	"	" — "
CALVO, JOSEPH M.	"	" —1804
BENITEZ, JOSEPH M.	"	" —1803
BENITEZ, A.	"	" —1802
BREUIL, FRANCIS.	San Domingo.	" — "
TRIGANT, THEODORE, A. B.	" "	" —1806
TRIGANT, LATOUR.	" "	" — "
ARMONA.	Havana.	" —1803
SANCHEZ, P.	"	" — "
SERRA.	"	" — "
BRUNELOT.	San Domingo.	" —1804
ORBE, GABRIEL DE.	Havana.	" —1803
CALDERON, N.	Porto Rico.	" — "
CARDENAS, NICHOLAS.	Havana.	" — "
CARDENAS, MANUEL.	"	" — "
CHACON.	"	" — "
CHACON.	"	" — "
CHACON.	"	" — "
MUÑOZ, NICHOLAS.	"	" —1802
ESCOBAR, MICHEL.	"	" —1803
ESCOBAR, JOSEPH M.	"	" — "
ESCARTI, GABRIEL.	"	" — "
ZAMORA, PEDRO.	"	1802—1805
GRANDCHAMP.	San Domingo.	" —1804

MOST REV. WILLIAM DU BOURG, D. D.,
Founder and First President of St. Mary's College.

NAME.	RESIDENCE.	ENTRY AND DEPARTURE.
POCHON.	San Domingo.	1802—1805
CAZEAUX, P.	" "	" — "
BAUDUY, F.	" "	" —1804
JARLÉ.	" "	" —1805
JARLÉ.	" "	" — "
MENON, JULES DE, A. B.	Paris.	" —1806
ESPINOSE, JULE D'.	San Domingo.	" —1807
LAFITTEAU.	" "	" —1804
MENARD.	" "	" —1805
DELISLE, COUPÉ.	" "	" — "
VERRIER, JULES.	" "	" —1804
LUBIN, ST. JULIEN.	" "	" —1806
BRAUD, JAMES.	" "	" —1807
NOUVEL, STANISLAS.	" "	" — "
VOLANT.	" "	" —1805
KEATING, JEROME.	Wilmington.	" —1806
HERNANDEZ, FRANCIS.	Havana.	1803—1805
LIPP, JAMES.	Hanover, Pa.	" — ?
O'BRIAN.	Maryland.	" — ?
BERQUIN, DU PARC.	San Domingo.	" —1807
DE MARBAUD, TERRELORGUE.	" "	" —1808
DUCATEL, JULES.	Baltimore.	" —1811
CLARK.	Lancaster.	" — ?
WILSON, ROBERT.	Baltimore.	" —1807
BURNS.	Ireland.	" — ?
BRENT, ROBERT.	Washington.	" —1806
DIGGES, DUDLEY.	"	" —1807
OLIVER, CHARLES.	Baltimore.	" —1811
JOHNSON, WILLIAM.	"	1804—1808
CAIN, RICHARD.	New York.	" —1807
COOKE, GEORGE.	Baltimore.	" — "
POTTER, SAMUEL.	"	" — "
CAMPBELL, HEND.	"	" —1806
STERRETT, WILLIAM, A. B.	"	" —1810
GRUNDY, BYRON.	"	" —1807
RIDDELL, ALEXANDER.	"	" —1808
DALRYMPLE, WILLIAM.	"	" —1807

NAME.	RESIDENCE.	ENTRY AND DEPARTURE.
OWINGS, BEALE.	Maryland.	1804—1805
CHAMPAGNE, HENRY.	Baltimore.	" —1811
RIDGELY, JOHN.	"	" —1808
SMITH, JASPER YEATES.	Lancaster.	" — "
ROGERS, FRANK.	Baltimore.	" — "
BERNABEU, JOHN.	"	" —1805
ROBB, CHARLES.	"	" — "
WILSON, GEORGE.	"	" — "
MOORE, THOMAS.	"	" —1805
CRAIG, JAMES.	Philadelphia.	" — "
LYNCH, HENRY.	New York.	" —1807
LIVINGSTON.	"	" —1806
MCCALL, JOHN.	Baltimore.	" —1810
DESHAUTEURS.	"	" —1805
SMITH, JOSEPH J.	?	" —1807
DORSEY, HILL.	?	" —1808
DORSEY, HAMMOND.	?	" — "
MORRIS, THOMAS A.	New York.	" —1806
LALANE, PAUL.	?	" —1809
LALANE, PETER.	?	" — "
IMBERT, RAPHAEL.	Havana.	" —1808
MAYO, EDWARD.	?	" —1806
LASALINIERE.	Guadaloupe.	" —1807
DOUILLARD.	"	? —1809
LATROBE, HENRY, A. B.	Middlesex, Eng.	1804—1808
PAUL, MICHAEL.	Guadaloupe.	" —1811
GODEFROI, LOUIS.	?	" —1808
MACOMB, DAVID.	?	" —1810
ARCAMBAL, BENJAMIN.	?	" —1808
ARCAMBAL, FELIX.	?	" — "
RANDOLPH, MANUEL.	?	" —1805
DE PESTRE, EDMOND.	?	" — ?
PATTERSON, EDWARD.	Baltimore.	" —1806
LORMAN, ALEXANDER.	"	" —1811
HALL, CALEB.	"	" —1807
GIBSON, JOHN.	"	" —1806
LEMMON.	?	" —1805

STUDENTS OF ST. MARY'S COLLEGE.

NAME.	RESIDENCE.	ENTRY AND DEPARTURE.
McHenry, James.	?	1804—1808
Schaeffer, William.	Baltimore.	" —1806
Cunningham.	?	" —1805
Martin, John.	Baltimore.	" —1809
Pascault, Francis.	?	? — "
Carroll, James.	Baltimore.	" —1808
Carroll, Henry, A. B.	"	" —1810
Oliver, Henry.	"	" — "
Ridgely, Edward, A. B.	"	" —1808
Eichelberger, Louis.	"	" —1810
Wilson, William.	?	" —1811
McMurtrie, Henry.	?	" —1809
Williamson, David.	Baltimore.	" —1805
Du Pavillon, Charles, A. B.	Guadeloupe.	" —1810
Keener.	?	" —1805
Worlock, Charles.	?	" — "
Robin, Edward.	?	" — "
Hollingsworth, Jacob.	Baltimore.	" —1807
Hollingsworth, Samuel.	"	" — "
Le Ray, Alexander.	?	" —1806
Murray, John.	?	" —1805
Hampton, John.	Philadelphia.	1804—1806 or 7
Macomb, Henry, A. B.	New York.	1804—1809
Macomb, Charles.	?	" —1807
Pierce, Levi, A. B.	York Co., Pa.	1805—1812
Williams, Otho.	Baltimore.	" —1805
Bayard, Richard.	?	" —1811
Milligan, George.	?	" — "
Tureau, Anatole.	?	" —1806
Conkling, Thomas.	?	" —1807
Vandyke, Nicholas.	?	" —1805
Johnson, Rinaldo.	?	" —1806
Ramsey, William.	Baltimore.	" —1809
Biays, Philip.	"	" —1807
Pratt, Edmond.	Philadelphia.	" —1806
Van Wyck, John Charles.	?	" —1808
Swan, John.	Baltimore.	" —1807

SEMINARY OF ST. SULPICE.

NAME.	RESIDENCE.	ENTRY AND DEPARTURE.
McFadon, John.	Baltimore.	1805—1809
Fite, Henry.	"	" —1806
Smith, John J.	"	" —1807
Reinicker, Samuel.	"	" —1805
Williams, James.	?	" —1808
Beck, Samuel.	?	" —1806
Meeker, Henry H.	?	" —1807
Feterel, François.	Baltimore.	" —1808
Des Sources, Vidalot.	?	" —1807
Kenhard, Richard.	?	" —1806
Kenhard, William.	?	" — "
Pierce, Edward.	?	" —1808
Barton, Edward, A. B.	England.	" —1812
Tureau, Emma.	?	" —1806
Morancy, P. Honoré.	?	" ?
Clérac, Auguste.	Guadeloupe.	" —1808
Le Febvre.	?	" —1806
Chassaing, Adolphe.	?	" —1811
Ryan, John.	?	" —1806
Lynch, Jasper, A. B.	New York.	" —1807
Kermantin, Coupé.	?	" — ?
Frigière, Louis.	?	" — ?
Chew, Benjamin.	?	" —1806
Ducatel, Jules.	Baltimore.	" —1811
Haynaud, F.	?	" — ?
Lynah.	?	" — ?
Bayard, Richard.	?	" — ?
Leaumont, Robert, A. B.	?	1806—1812
Sewall, Robert, A. B.	Maryland.	" — "
Sewall, William, A. B.	"	" —1813
Tuite, Henry.	?	" —1814
Coleman, Thomas, A. M.	Lancaster, Pa.	" —1812
Davis, Frederick.	Boston.	" — "
Davis, Horatio, A. B.	"	" — "
Harris, John.	?	" —1814
Meuillon, Benjamin.	?	" — ?
Sims, Woodrop, A. B.	Philadelphia.	" —1813
Suquet, Lewis.	?	" —1812

NAME.	RESIDENCE.	ENTRY AND DEPARTURE.
WISE, JOHN.	?	1806— ?
LONGUEVILLE, SEVERE.	?	" —1813
THOMSON, JAMES, A. B.	New York.	1807—1815
PROWELL, WILLIAM.	?	" —1811
BUMBERRY, HENRY.	?	" — "
BOISGERARD, EDWARD.	?	" — ?
VINCENDON, CHARLES.	?	" —1812
ST. CERGUES, GEORGE, A. B.	Martinique.	" —1814
CHANCEL, CHARLES.	?	1808— ?
MILLIGAN, JOHN.	?	" —1811
LUDSON, JAMES HENRY.	?	" —1813
DESGATIERES, ALFRED.	?	" —1814
LAGRANGE, ARTHUR.	Pittsburgh.	" —1813
ROSS, GEORGE, A. B.	New Orleans.	" — "
ROSS, ROBERT.	" "	" — "
DURAND, CASIMIR.	?	" — "
DALE, RICHARD.	?	" —1812
DALE, MONTGOMERY.	?	" — ?
MULLER, EDWARD.	?	" —1814
ST. MARTIN, W., A. B.	Martinique.	" —1816
ST. MARTIN, GEORGE.	?	" — ?
RAPHAEL, AMÉDÉE.	?	" —1811
MIDDLETON, THOMAS, A. B.	Charleston, S. C.	" —1816
DESPOINTES, NELSON.	?	" —1812
CATALOGNE, AUGUSTUS.	?	" —1814
CATALOGNE, GUSTAVE.	?	" — ?
CHAMPAGNE, H. J.	Baltimore.	" —1811
MONTEIRO, PETER.	?	" — ?
COUPER, SAMUEL H.	?	" — ?
RIDDLE, JAMES.	?	" — ?
READ, BEDFORD.	?	" —1811
COAKLEY, WILLIAM.	?	" —1814
SINNOTT, J., A. M.	Dublin.	" — ?
MCHENRY, J., A. M.	Baltimore.	" —1808
SMITH, J., A. M.	Lancaster, Pa.	? — "
MORGAN, W.	?	" — ?
SITGREAVES, W., A. B.	Pennsylvania.	1809—1813

NAME.	RESIDENCE.	ENTRY AND DEPARTURE.
GUTIÉRES DEL KIBERO, VAL.	Caraccos.	1800— ?
ELWES, ALFRED.	?	" — ?
KELLY, GEORGE.	?	" — ?
KELLY, EDWARD.	?	" — ?
CARROLL, HENRY, A. B.	Hagerstown.	" —1812
MOREAU, MICHEL.	?	" —1813
RIDGELY, LAMING.	Baltimore.	" — "
RIOLS, BARTHELEMY.	?	" — "
TUFTS, W.	?	" —1812
SPALDING, JAMES.	?	" — ?
ST. CERGUES, GUSTAVE.	?	" — ?
ALLAIN, SOSTHENE.	?	" — ?
WATERS, JOSEPH.	?	" — ?
DIDIER, EDMUND.	?	" —1813
PREVOST, AIMÉ.	?	" — ?
PREVOST, BENJAMIN.	?	" — ?
McQUINN, JOHN.	?	" —1815
TIERNAN, CHARLES.	?	" —1816
HOWARD, WILLIAM, A. M.	Baltimore.	" —1811
PATILLA, HENRY.	?	" — ?
DESPODA, CHARLES.	?	" — ?
BERNABEU, JOHN.	?	" — ?
CLANZEL, JOSEPH.	?	" —1809
CHAMBELLAN, LOUIS.	?	" —1810
CAMPBELL, DANIEL.	?	" — "
COURET, JOSEPH.	?	" — "
COURCEY, WILLIAM.	?	" — "
GOUGE, HYP. DE.	?	" — "
GOUGE, AMACH. DE.	?	" — "
DESPOINTES, NELSON.	?	" — "
DESPOINTES, A.	?	" — "
EICKELBERGER, LEWIS, A. M.	?	" — "
FENNEL, MAURICE.	?	" — "
FRIEGIÈRE, JOHN.	?	" — "
FERRÉRE, JOHN.	?	" — "
GIRARD, VINCENT.	?	" — "
GIBBON, JOHN.	?	" —1809

NAME.	RESIDENCE.	ENTRY AND DEPARTURE.
LALANNE, PAUL.	?	1809— ?
LALANNE, PETER.	?	" — ?
HOSKINS, RICHARD.	?	" —1811
HASKINS, HENRY.	?	" — "
HAIGH, SAMUEL.	?	" —1810
LEE, HENRY.	?	" — "
LIVERS, ERASTUS.	?	" —1810
MACOMB, HENRY.	?	" — "
MACOMB, CHARLES.	?	" — "
MONTEIRO, PETER.	?	" —1811
McCALL, JOHN.	?	" — "
OLIVER, HENRY.	?	" —1810
OLIVER, CHARLES.	?	" —1812
PAUL, MICHAEL.	?	" —1810
PRATT, EDWIN.	?	" — "
PESCAYE, JULES.	?	" —1811
SULLIVAN, T.	?	" — ?
STERLING, WILLIAM.	?	" —1810
STERLING, RUFUS.	?	" — "
SHERMAN, EDWARD.	?	" — ?
SHERMAN, UZEIL.	?	" — ?
SPADA, CHARLES.	?	" —1811
WILSON, WILLIAM.	?	" —1810
WILSON, EDWARD.	?	" — "
WATERS, JAMES.	?	" —1811
SOSTHENE, ALLAIN.	?	1810— ?
STERETT, GEORGE.	?	" —1814
ALLEGRIA, DIEGO.	?	" —1815
SEGHERS, JULIEN, A. B.	New Orleans.	" —1814
VERGARA, AUGUSTIN.	?	" —1813
DESPINVILLE, CHARLES.	?	" — "
BASSORA, JOSEPH.	?	" —1815
MAUNY, J. B.	?	" —1813
CHASSAIN, EDWARD.	?	" —1814
JACKSON, EBENEZER.	?	" —1813
AQUART, CHARLES.	?	" —1812
AQUART, AUGUST.	?	" — "

NAME.	RESIDENCE.	ENTRY AND DEPARTURE.
DERIVEAN, DEVILLE.	?	1810—1815
BERTRAND, PIERRE.	?	" — "
BERTRAND, JEAN.	?	" — "
COAKLEY, JAMES.	?	" —1814
SAUNIER, G.	?	" — "
TAYLOR, RICHARD.	?	" —1812
VILA, SALVADOR.	?	" — ?
FRENCH, JOHN.	?	" — ?
LORMAN, ALEXANDER.	?	" — ?
WISE, JOHN.	?	" — ?
PATTERSON, HENRY.	?	" —1814
PATTERSON, GEORGE.	?	" — "
SEGHERS, JULIEN, A. B.	New Orleans.	" — "
PATTERSON, HENRY.	?	" — "
RITCHIE, ARCHIBALD.	?	" —1812
FISHER, WILLIAM, A. M.	Baltimore.	" — "
MILLAN, JOHN.	?	" — ?
MILLAN, LEO.	?	" — ?
DIDIER, FRANKLIN.	?	" —1812
VON ALPHEN, JOHN.	?	" —1813
VON ALPHEN, ANTHONY.	?	" — "
DALL, JOHN.	?	" —1812
LATOUR, HENRY.	?	" —1810
KIMMEL, ANTHONY.	?	? — ?
DECKER, JACOB.	?	1810—1812
FORNEY, MATHIAS.	?	" — "
BABY, EUGENE.	?	" — ?
SUMMERWELLS, HENRY.	?	" —1811
SAVARY, ALPHONSE.	Baltimore.	" — ?
SAVARY, RICHARD.	"	" — ?
STEWART, RICHARD.	?	" —1815
PATTERSON, GEORGE.	?	" — ?
WOLFF, PETER,	?	" — ?
CARROLL, CH.	Baltimore.	" —1815
HOLLAND, NATHANIEL.	?	" — ?
TODD, F. P.	?	" — ?
SWAN, GEORGE.	?	" — ?

STUDENTS OF ST. MARY'S COLLEGE.

NAME.	RESIDENCE.	ENTRY AND DEPARTURE.
O'Donnell, Columbus.	?	1810— ?
Dormin, W.	?	" — ?
Milhan, Lewis.	?	" — ?
Milhan, John.	?	" — ?
Bernabeu, Ch., A. B.	Baltimore.	1811— ?
Waters, James.	?	" —1811
Emory, Richard.	?	" —1815
Mummey, Independence.	?	" — ?
Couper, James.	?	" — ?
Hook, Lewis.	?	" —1812
Hackley, James.	?	" — ?
Patterson, Octavus.	?	" —1814
Winn, John.	?	" —1813
Belmont, Francis.	?	" — "
Bartholemew, John.	?	" — ?
Clarence, Alexander.	?	" — ?
Bennet, Harry.	?	" —1818
Leclerc, Lucien.	?	" — ?
Styger, William Tell.	?	" — ?
Usher, James.	?	" —1812
Timon, J.	?	" — ?
Hollingsworth, Ho.	?	" — ?
Dornin, Thomas.	?	" — ?
Dornin, William.	?	" — ?
Leigh, George S.	?	" — ?
Raphel, Amedee.	?	" — ?
Contee, John.	?	" — ?
Ducatel, Hyp.	?	" — ?
Gibert.	?	" — ?
Hackley, John.	?	" — ?
Minor, John, A. M.	Virginia.	" —1814
Valladares, Juan.	?	" — "
Escardo, Pedro.	?	" — "
Chappotin, Charles.	Havana.	" —1816
Paca, William Bennett.	Maryland.	" —1812
Sterling, John.	New Orleans.	" —1818
Serra, Felix M.	Havana.	" —1816

SEMINARY OF ST. SULPICE.

NAME.	RESIDENCE.	ENTRY AND DEPARTURE.
SERRA, PABLO MARIA.	Havana.	1811—1816
SANTANA, JUAN N.	?	" —1814
MORALES, JOSÉ S.	?	" — "
DESMARAIS, ANTOINE VASSAL.	?	" — ?
DESMARAIS, S.	?	" — ?
CATALOGNE, CHARLES.	?	" —1815
PAPIN, THEOBALD.	?	" — "
SOUDON, CHARLES.	Martinique.	" —1816
GALLET, L.	"	" —1818
ST. CLAIR, L.	?	" — ?
PALLU, G.	?	" —1813
DESGATIÉRES, S.	?	" —1814
KERR, ELIE W.	?	" —1813
SEGHERS, EDWARD.	New Orleans.	" —1815
GIBSON, JOHN.	?	" — ?
DUCATEL, HYP.	?	" —1816
CARROLL, HENRY.	?	" —1814
LEFEVRE, VICTORIN.	?	" —1813
GARNETT, JAMES M.	?	" —1812
CARROLL, CHARLES.	Hagerstown.	" —1813
GIROUST, AMÉDÉE.	?	" —1815
BACOMOIS, AMÉDÉE.	?	" —1813
GUESTIER, CHARLES.	?	1812—1818
JOVAR, FLORENCE.	?	" —1813
VERGARA, A.	?	" — "
ROSSETER, JOHN.	?	" —1812
MOSHER, JAMES.	?	" —1814
DAVIS, OSCAR.	?	" —1812
LAUTNER, PEDRO.	?	" — "
ARANZAMONDI, JOSÉ NICOLAS.	?	" — ?
LEFÉVRE, VICTORIN.	?	" —1813
GEOFFROY, JOHN PASCHAL.	San Domingo.	" — "
ROMAN, SOSTHENE.	?	" —1812
DRAKE, CARLOS.	?	" —1814
PURVIANCE, ROBERT.	Baltimore.	" —1818
CLARK, ROBERT.	?	" — ?
PERKINS, THOMAS.	?	" —1813

STUDENTS OF ST. MARY'S COLLEGE.

NAME.	RESIDENCE.	ENTRY AND DEPARTURE
CARROLL, CHARLES.	Baltimore.	1812—1815
TAILLANDIER.	?	" — ?
GUBERNATOR, J. L., A. B.	Pennsylvania.	1812
DAVIS, H., A. B.	Philadelphia.	1811—1812
SENZERQUE.	?	1812— ?
BIDDELL, ROBERT.	?	" —1817
BUCKLER, JOHN.	?	" — ?
WALSH, CHARLES.	?	" —1818
LAMBERT, WILLIAM.	?	" — ?
ELLICOTT, JAMES.	?	" —1812
DESPADA, CHARLES.	?	" — ?
LAROQUE, VICTOR.	?	" — ?
COAKLEY, JAMES.	?	" —1814
LAROQUE, EDWARD.	?	" — ?
BARTHOLOMÉ, THOMAS.	?	" — ?
BARTHOLOMÉ, JOSEPH.	?	" — ?
BYRNE, COLUMBUS.	?	" —1813
BYRNE, PATRICK.	?	" — "
CARROLL, WILLIAM.	?	" — "
DAVIDGE, F. H.	?	? — ?
DESMOYER.	?	? — ?
HOWARD, JAMES, A. M.	Baltimore.	1812—1815
BYRNE, H. A., A. B.	Pennsylvania.	1813
CARELLE, WILLIAM.	?	1812— ?
DAVIS, OSCAR.	?	" — ?
WHEELER, MICHAEL, A. M.	Baltimore.	1813—1818
WARNER, MICHAEL.	?	" — "
VASSAL, ANTOINE DESMARAIS.	Trinidad.	" —1817
ALCALA, J. L. DE.	?	" —1813
BONAPARTE, JEROME NAP.	Baltimore.	" —1814
RUSSELL, GEORGE ROBERT.	?	" — ?
BEYLEY, MICHAEL.	Porto Rico.	" — ?
DONNELL, JOHN SMITH.	Baltimore.	" — ?
DONNELL, JAMES ISAAC.	"	" — ?
CARROLL, HENRY, A. B.	Hagerstown.	" —1813
PATTERSON, HENRY.	?	" — ?

NAME.	RESIDENCE.	ENTRY AND DEPARTURE.
STEWART, RICHARD.	Baltimore.	1813— ?
AGUIRE, PEDRO JOSÉ.	?	" —1814
CHASSAING, ADOLPHE.	?	" — ?
DE CATALOGNE, GUSTAVE.	?	" — ?
DE CATALOGNE, A.	?	" —1814
DALE, JOHN.	?	" — ?
DORFEY, ROBERT.	?	" —1815
DESPOINTES, NELSON.	?	" —1814
KAVANAGH, EDWARD.	?	" — ?
MOREAU, MICHAEL.	?	" —1813
MIDDLETON, THOMAS, A. B.	Charleston, S. C.	" —1816
SMITH, SAMUEL.	?	" —1815
DE ST. CLAIR, LEOPOLD.	?	" — "
ST. MARTIN, GEORGE.	Baltimore.	" —1816
ST. MARTIN, WILLIAM, A. B.	"	" — "
SERRA, FELIX.	Havana.	" — "
HORN, CHARLES R.	?	" — ?
SPEAR, WILLIAM.	Baltimore.	" — ?
SMITH, SAMUEL.	?	" — ?
DIX, JOHN E.	?	" — ?
WARNER, M.	?	" — ?
O'DONNELL, JOHN.	?	" —1817
O'DONNELL, ELLIOT.	?	" —1814
O'DONNELL, SMITH.	?	" — "
ROMAN, ANDRÉ BIENVENU, A. B.	New Orleans.	" —1815
ZERINGUE, CAMILLE, A. B.	Louisiana.	" — "
ECCLESTON, SAMUEL, A. M.	?	" —1819
ROBINSON, ALEXANDER.	?	" — ?
STERRETT, GEORGE.	?	" — ?
MAGRUDER, ENOCH.	Maryland.	" — ?
DORFEY, ROBERT.	?	" — ?
MOSHER, JAMES, A. M.	Baltimore.	" —1814
KREBS, W. GEORGE.	?	" —1818
SLOAN, JAMES.	?	" —1814
JACKSON, E., A. B.	Savannah.	" — ?
LAUMONT, R., A. B.	Charleston.	" —1814
SAUNIER, G., A. B.	San Domingo.	" — "

Rt. Rev. Simon G. Bruté, D. D.,
First Bishop of Vincennes.

STUDENTS OF ST. MARY'S COLLEGE.   93

NAME.	RESIDENCE.	ENTRY AND DEPARTURE.
WALSH, C., A. B.	Baltimore.	1813—1815
BARRY, JOHN, A. B.	"	1814—1824
BARRY, ROBERT.	?	" —1818
BERNABEU, ALONZO.	?	" —1819
CARRÉRE, ROBERT.	Baltimore.	" —1815
DESGATIÉRES, STEPHEN.	?	" —1814
DUVAL, JOHN.	?	" —1817
LEROY, LOUIS WILLIAM, A. B.	Washington, N. C.	" —1820
LYNAH, EDWARD THOMAS.	Charleston.	" —1818
MAGRUDER, ENOCH.	?	" —1816
PURVIANCE, HUGH.	Baltimore.	" — "
PURVIANCE, WILSON.	"	" — "
RUTLEDGE, EDWARD.	Charleston.	" —1818
RIDGELY, RICHARD.	?	" —1815
STEWART, RICHARD.	?	" — "
VESPRE, FIS.	?	" — "
RINGGOLD, JOSEPH.	?	" —1814
SINNOT, W.	Baltimore.	" — ?
ALEXANDER, EDWARD.	Virginia.	1815—1818
ANDREWS, ROBERT.	Bordeaux.	" —1817
BERGRASS, PIERRE.	Sta Lucia Island.	" —1819
BREASHEAR, WILLIAM.	?	" —1816
CARRERE, EDWARD.	Baltimore.	" —1818
CARRERE, JOHN.	"	" —1819
CANAL, J. B.	Teneriffe.	" —1816
CHESTON, JAMES.	Baltimore.	" —1821
CHAPHAM, JAMES.	"	" —1819
DE BUTTS, THESSELIUS.	?	" —1820
DUCATEL, CAMILE.	Baltimore.	" —1818
DUCATEL, EMILE.	"	" — "
DIXON, JAMES.	?	" —1815
DONALSON, WILLIAM.	Baltimore.	" —1820
DONALSON, ALEXANDER.	"	" —1822
ELLICOTT, ANDREW.	"	" —1818
ELLICOTT, JAMES.	"	" —1820
McFADON, JAMES.	"	" —1819
GILL, DANIEL.	"	" —1820

NAME.	RESIDENCE.	ENTRY AND DEPARTURE.
HOWARD, CHARLES.	Baltimore.	1815—1819
HILL, WILLIAM.	?	" —1816
HOFFMAN, FRANCIS.	Baltimore.	" —1817
HOFFMAN, SAMUEL.	"	" —1818
HAMILTON, HAWKINS.	"	" — "
KREBS, CH. WARNER.	"	" —1819
HAWKINS, H.	?	" —1818
MCKIM, JOHN, A. M.	Ireland.	" —1815
MEREDITH, THOMAS.	Baltimore.	" —1818
M'GUIRE.	?	" —1816
OGLE, W.	Baltimore.	" —1819
PADILLA, MANUEL.	?	" —1815
PARMENTIER, CHARLES THEO.	Philadelphia.	" —1816
ROBINSON, ARCHIBALD.	?	" —1816
ROSSEAU, RODOLPHE.	Louisiana.	" —1819
ROMAN, JAMES TELESPHORE.	?	" —1818
SEGHERS, THEODORE.	Brussels.	" —1819
SEGHERS, ADOLPHE, A. B.	"	" —1820
SEGHERS, VICTOR.	"	" —1821
STEWART, DAVID.	Baltimore.	" —1816
STUMP, W.	Harford Co., Md.	" —1817
WILLIAMSON, ADOLPHE.	?	" —1819
WILLIAMSON, CHARLES.	Baltimore.	" —1817
WILLIAMSON, GEORGES.	?	" —1818
WALTER, PETER.	?	" —1816
DONALDSON, WILLIAM, A. B.	Baltimore.	" —1822
ALEXANDER, E., A. M.	Virginia.	" —1818
RUTLEDGE, E. A., A. B.	Charleston, S. C.	" —1818
WALSH, C., A. M.	?	" —1815
ALLAIN, CHARLES.	?	1816—1817
BUWAL, HENRY.	Baltimore.	" — "
BRENNAN, PRE. OLIVER.	?	" — "
MCBLAIR, LYDE GOODWIN.	?	" —1823
COOPER, S.	?	" —1817
CONOLY.	?	" —1818
CARROLL, CHARLES.	Carrollton, Md.	" —1817
DUGHAN, COMB.	?	" —1818

NAME.	RESIDENCE.	ENTRY AND DEPARTURE.
DIDIER, FERDINAND.	?	1816—1818
DE CLARY, HENRY.	Pittsburgh.	" —1817
DAWSON, FREDERICK.	England.	" —1820
DAWSON, PHILIP.	"	" — "
GREETHAN, JOHN.	Baltimore.	" —1818
HEWIT, R.	?	" —1819
HILLEN, J.	?	" —1818
HEWIT, ELY.	?	" —1820
HOLLINGSWORTH, JESSE.	Baltimore.	" —1819
HOLLINGSWORTH, JOHN.	"	" —1818
HAYES, EDWARD.	"	" —1817
LEYPAULD, FREDERICK.	"	" —1820
LECLERC, LOUIS.	?	" —1818
LANDRY, TRASIMOND.	?	" —1819
MARIS, MATHIAS.	?	" —1817
MAILLARD, PHILOGENE.	?	" —1821
NORRIS, W.	?	" —1816
NORRIS, RICHARD.	?	" — "
NORRIS, EDWARD.	?	" — "
OLIVER, THOMAS.	?	" —1818
PETER, JESSE.	Baltimore.	" — ?
POLK, GILLES.	"	" —1819
RIDGELY, CHARLES GEORGE.	Dover, Del.	" —1821
ROY, JAMES P.	Virginia.	" —1818
RAFFERTY, FELIX.	San Domingo.	" —1817
RIDGELY, WILLIAM.	Baltimore.	" —1819
RIDGELY, JAMES.	"	" — "
RICHARDSON, ROBERT.	?	" — "
SMITH, SAMUEL.	?	" —1818
TAYLOR, ALEXANDER.	?	" —1817
THOMSON, W.	Baltimore.	" —1818
VAIL, CHARLES.	France.	" —1817
VAIL, EDWARD.	"	" —1818
VANPRADELLES, BENEDICT.	?	" —1817
WIKOFF, DANIEL.	New Orleans.	" — "
WEST, BENJAMIN.	Baltimore.	" —1822
WEST, WILLIAM.	"	" —1821

NAME.	RESIDENCE.	ENTRY AND DEPARTURE.
WHELAN, WILLIAM.	?	1816— ?
ZERINGUE, J.	New Orleans.	" —1820
STIRLING.	Louisiana.	" — ?
CONNOLLY, RICHARD.	Ireland.	" — ?
GUESTIER, CHARLES.	Bordeaux.	" — ?
SPEARE, WILLIAM.	Baltimore.	" — ?
DUNOVERS, JUSTIN.	San Domingo.	" — ?
DE CHAPOTIN, C., A. M.	Savannah.	" —1816
DIDIER, F. J., A. M.	Baltimore.	1816—1818
MAGENDER, E.	Maryland.	? —1816
RIDGELY, E. G., A. M.	Delaware.	1816—1821
WILLIAMSON, G., A. M.	Baltimore.	1815— ?
DAWSON, F., A. B.	England.	1816—1820
BEND, HENRY.	?	1817—1817
BLAND, W.	?	" — "
BLAND, J.	?	" — "
CHATTARD, HENRY.	Baltimore.	" —1820
McCANNAN, JOHN.	?	" —1818
COSKREY, W.	?	" —1822
COREA.	?	" —1819
DE PESTRE, JULIEN.	?	" — "
LA FERTÉ, JEAN.	?	" — "
DUCKET, JUDSON.	Baltimore.	" —1820
ELWES, HENRY.	?	" —1818
FREMONT, BENJAMIN.	Baltimore.	" —1822
FINISTER, ALEXANDER.	?	" — ?
HARRIS, EDWARD.	?	" —1820
JENKINS, FRANCIS.	?	" — "
KOBERSTON, ROBERT.	?	" —1818
LONG OR LANY, ANDREW.	?	" — "
MAYERS.	?	" — ?
PRESTMAN, W.	?	" —1819
ROMAN, VICTOR.	Louisiana.	" —1823
ROMAN, MICHEL.	New Orleans.	" — "
ROMON, JUSTINIEN.	" "	" —1826
ROMON, JEAN JACQUES, A. B.	" "	" —1818
RAMBEAU, GILBERT.	?	" —1819

STUDENTS OF ST. MARY'S COLLEGE.

NAME.	RESIDENCE.	ENTRY AND DEPARTURE.
Stenson, William.	Baltimore.	1817—1828
Scott, Parker.	?	" —1819
Rutelge, H. A., A. B.	Charleston, S. C.	" —1822
Tiernan, Luke.	Baltimore.	" —1819
Tiernan, William.	"	" —1822
Torrices, Antonio.	?	" —1817
Williamson, William.	?	" —1822
Warner, Georges, Sr.	?	" —1819
Warner, Georges, Jr.	?	? — ?
Whelan, W.	?	? — ?
Savary, Lewis.	?	1817—1824
Bruce, H.	?	1818— ?
Bruce, Robert.	?	" —1819
Beatty, James.	?	" —1821
Cox, James, A. B.	Baltimore.	" —1820
Cornegham, John.	?	" —1819
Desmoyer.	?	1818
Delavigne, E.	?	1818— "
Dugan, Lewis H.	Baltimore.	" — ?
Dobler, Daniel.	"	" — ?
Elliot H.	?	" —1820
De Frias, Antonio.	Havana.	" —1819
Gleen.	?	" —1817
Keerls, William.	?	" —1822
Leynold, William.	?	" — ?
Latrobe, Henry, A. B.	Baltimore.	" —1819
Mitchell, James.	"	" —1822
Nenninger, Benjamin.	?	" —1818
Padilla, Joseph.	?	" — ?
Robinson, Robert.	Baltimore.	1818
Smith, John.	?	1818— "
Triese.	?	" —1819
White, J.	?	" —1821
White, Charles J.	Baltimore.	" —1823
Chance, J.	?	" —1818
Lavigne, E.	?	" —1820
Drake, J.	?	" — "

NAME.	RESIDENCE.	ENTRY AND DEPARTURE.
DRAKE, F.	?	1818—1820
MEREDITH, J.	Baltimore.	" —1823
DICKEHUT.	Baltimore.	" —1820
BARRY, JOHN.	?	" —1824
CHATARD, FREDERICK.	Baltimore.	" —1820
VOLDOR, JOSEPH.	?	" — "
PONCET.	?	" —1821
HANAHAN, ROSS.	North Carolina.	" — "
HARRIS, E.	Baltimore.	" —1820
HALL, F.	"	" —1823
LANDRY, C.	?	" — ?
ROSSEAU, S.	?	" —1823
HORN, J.	?	" —1819
LANDRY, C.	?	" —1818
DE FRIAS, ANTONIO.	Havana.	" —1824
McBLAIR, WILLIAM, A. B.	Baltimore.	" —1823
ELLIOTT, HENRY.	?	" —1820
SCHARTZE, E.	?	" —1819
SCHARTZE, JAMES.	?	" — "
BEDFORD, G.	?	" —1820
BARRY, D.	Baltimore.	" —1827
WARING, JOHN.	?	1819—1821
SMITH, W.	?	" —1819
MUÑOS, MANUEL.	?	" —1823
MUÑOS, RAPHAEL.	?	" — "
MOSHER, EDWARD.	?	" —1820
WHELAN, W.	?	" —1823
INGLIS, W.	?	" —1820
WILLIAMSON, A.	Baltimore.	" — "
BRENNAN, AD.	"	" —1822
BRENNAN, EDWARD.	"	" — "
McNAIR, R.	North Carolina.	" —1821
MAYERS, H.	?	" —1827
WHITE, C. S.	Baltimore.	" —1825
WILLIAMSON, JOSEPH.	?	" — "
BRENNAN, EDWARD.	?	" —1823
XIMENES, ANT.	Havana.	" —1824

NAME.	RESIDENCE.	ENTRY AND DEPARTURE.
WELLS, W.	?	1819—1820
BARNEY, C.	?	" —1821
WALSH, J. S.	?	" —1820
ROBINSON.	?	" — "
FREISE, HENRY.	?	" — "
LOWERY, EN.	Baltimore.	" —1823
MCLEANE, ADAM.	"	" — "
BOWIE, WILLIAM.	?	" —1820
GEGAN, JOSEPH.	?	" — "
STEVENSON.	?	" — ?
BRUCE, N.	?	" —1820
BRUCE, HENRY.	?	" — "
LEMOINE, F.	?	" — "
FRIEZE, H.	?	" —1824
STEVENSON, WILLIAM.	?	" —1825
HAWSKINS, JOHN.	?	" —1824
WEST, J.	?	" — "
MARYÉ, BRANTZ.	?	" —1827
COCKEY, CHARLES.	?	" —1825
WARFIELD, W.	?	" — "
IGLEHEART, JOSEPH.	?	" —1824
HOLLINS, Fs.	?	" — ?
CAVENAUGH, E., A. M.	?	? —1819
SEGHERS, THEODORE, A. M.	?	? — "
PURVIANCE, R., A. M.	?	? — "
HOWARD, CHARLES, A. M.	?	? — "
SMITH, TS.	?	1819—1820
THOMAS.	?	" —1819
MOSHER.	?	" — "
RICAUD, J.	?	" — "
RICAUD, R.	?	" — "
HORN, JOHN.	Baltimore.	" — "
WHITE, B.	?	" —1821
TIERNAN, L.	?	" —1819
NOON, JOHN.	?	" — "
SMITH, GUSTAVE.	?	" —1820
HOLLINS, FRANCIS.	Baltimore.	" —1823

NAME.	RESIDENCE.	ENTRY AND DEPARTURE.
Butter, G.	?	1819—1821
Brance.	?	" —1820
Randoll, W.	?	" —1821
Brooke, R.	?	" —1819
Alcok, W.	?	" — "
Beaty, E.	?	" — ?
Wheeler, D.	?	" — ?
Dunbar, J.	Baltimore.	" — ?
Dunbar, W.	"	" —1820
McBlair, C.	?	" — ?
Hermange, F.	?	" —1821
Schroeder, H.	Baltimore.	" —1827
Maria, A.	?	" — ?
Thompson, J.	Baltimore.	" —1820
Bennett, H.	?	" — "
Williams, W.	?	" —1821
Gile, G. M., A. M.	Baltimore.	? —1820
Inglis, W., A. M.	"	? — "
Mezick, Thomas.	?	1820—1821
Night, Edward.	?	" —1825
Gaston, A.	North Carolina.	" —1823
De Butts, J. H.	Baltimore.	" — "
Price, Thomas.	"	" —1821
Favillon.	?	" — "
Winder, W.	Baltimore.	" — ?
Winder, Charles.	"	" — ?
Fossier, A.	?	" —1821
Haydel.	?	" — "
Armant, John.	?	" —1823
Scotti, F.	?	" —1820
Harang, M.	?	" —1821
Lucas, E.	Baltimore.	" — "
Ridgely, C.	?	" — "
Robinson, Albert.	?	" — "
Hoffman, A.	?	" —1823
Donnell, N.	?	" —1822
Lynch, E.	?	" —1821

NAME.	RESIDENCE.	ENTRY AND DEPARTURE.
LAMARHERE, THOMAS.	?	1820—1822
TAYLOR, WILLIAM.	?	" —1821
ZERINGUE, F.	?	" — "
MEREDITH, G.	?	" — "
ALEXANDER, ASHTON.	?	" — "
BURKER, JOHN.	?	" —1822
HOFFMAN, WILLIAM.	?	" — "
WINDER, WILLIAM.	Baltimore.	" —1824
LUCAS, EDWARD.	"	" —1825
TIERNAN, M.	?	" — ?
SINNOTT, W.	?	" —1825
BATHURST, JOHN.	?	" —1821
DONELL, N.	?	" —1820
VECCHIO, P.	?	" —1822
BAXLEY, WILLIAM.	?	" —1821
LAW, TH.	?	" —1820
BUCHANAN, JAMES.	?	" — "
WALTER.	?	" — "
MEREDITH, G.	?	" — "
WILLIAMS, JOSEPH.	?	" — "
TRAILEY, CHARLES.	Baltimore.	" —1822
BURKE, BARTH.	?	" —1821
PATTERSON, WILLIAM.	Baltimore.	" — "
PINKNEY, FREDERICK.	"	" —1822
PINKNEY, HENRY.	"	" — "
BOARMAN, CHARLES.	?	" —1821
ELLICOTT, WILLIAM.	?	" — "
CHANCHE, JAMES.	?	" — "
COULTER, WILLIAM.	?	" —1823
BEATTY, JOHN.	Baltimore.	" —1826
YOUNG, A.	?	" —1822
NORRIS, R.	?	" — "
NORRIS, G.	?	" —1821
WARNER, EDWARD.	?	" —1824
WARNER, A.	?	" — "
WARNER, G. K., A. M.	Baltimore.	" —1821
WELLMORE, N.	"	" —1823

NAME.	RESIDENCE.	ENTRY AND DEPARTURE.
Dugan, F.	?	1820—1821
Small, A.	?	" — "
Kelly, J.	?	" —1821
Smith, E.	?	" — "
Gross, L.	Baltimore.	" —1822
Cheston, G.	"	" —1823
Cheston, S.	"	" —1824
Smith, D.	?	" —1821
Berry, Daniel.	?	" — "
Kimmel, H.	?	" —1822
Norris, W.	?	" —1821
Polk, William.	?	" —1823
Smiley, Hamilton.	?	" —1821
Smith, John D.	?	" — "
Craig, John.	?	" — "
Merryman.	?	" — "
Southall.	?	" — "
Tiernan, H.	?	" — ?
Ellicot, Sl.	?	" —1822
Warfield, G.	?	" —1821
Colvin, H.	?	" —1823
Hollingworth, P.	?	" —1822
Dorsey, T.	Baltimore.	" — "
Pattison, John.	Scotland.	" —1821
Pattison, G.	"	" —1822
Pattison, Robert.	"	" —1822
Pattison, F.	"	" — "
Gregg.	?	" — "
Medina, Joseph.	Porto Rico.	" —1823
Edgerton, John.	Baltimore.	" —1824
Xaupi, Lewis.	?	" —1825
Winder, Charles.	?	" —1824
Burke, John.	Baltimore.	" —1823
Favignon, Lucien.	Matanzas.	" —1826
Morales, Toby.	?	1821—1821
Arismende, Bas.	?	1821 died Apr. 1821
Stephens, Gtray.	Baltimore.	1821—1823

STUDENTS OF ST. MARY'S COLLEGE.

NAME.	RESIDENCE.	ENTRY AND DEPARTURE.
ROBINSON, WILLIAM.	?	1821— ?
HAMMOND, RUBIN.	?	" —1822
KNIGHT, EDWARD A., A. M.	?	" —1823
MUDD, ATHANASIUS.	?	" — "
BOWIE, WILLIAM.	?	" — "
GHISLIN, RICHARD.	?	" — "
MATTOS.	?	" —1822
NEMINGER, B.	?	" — "
NEMINGER, JOHN.	?	" — "
MEADE, RICHARD.	?	" —1824
DE FRIAS, JOSEPH.	?	" —1826
GHISELIN, ROBERT.	Maryland.	" —1824
JENKINS, M.	Baltimore.	" —1821
ALCOCK, EDWARD, A. M.	"	" —1823
ELLIS, BARTH.	?	" —1821
TAYLOR, JOSEPH.	?	" —1822
FANESTORK, E.	Baltimore.	" — "
FANESTORK, CHARLES.	"	" — "
CARRY, EDWARD.	?	" —1821
MYERS, L.	Pennsylvania.	" —1822
MCKIM, WILLIAM.	Baltimore.	" —1825
MCKIM, ISAAC.	"	" —1827
WILLIAMS, JOHN.	?	" —1823
DALEY, JAMES.	?	" —1821
ROGERS, HENRY.	?	" — ?
CROSDALE, WILLIAM.	?	" —1823
CROSDALE, G.	?	" — ?
MEREDITH, G.	?	" —1822
FAVILLON.	?	" — "
WARNINGTON, EDWARD.	?	" — "
HARDEY.	?	" —1821
WALKER, WILLIAM.	?	" —1824
WALSH, YATES.	?	" — "
EDWARDS, W.	?	" — ?
BRISBEN.	?	" —1821
MICHAEL.	?	" — "
DONALSON, WILLIAM.	?	" — ?

NAME.	RESIDENCE.	ENTRY AND DEPARTURE.
Mezick.	Baltimore.	1821—1822
Knight, Edward.	"	" —1821
Campbell, James.	"	" —1824
Schultze, Henry.	"	" — ?
Dumbor, William.	?	" — ?
Dumbor, G.	?	? — ?
Jones, Caleb.	Baltimore.	1821—1826
Latrobe, B.	"	" —1823
Ricaud, Richard.	?	? — ?
Ricaud, James.	?	? — ?
Reyburn, J.	?	1821— ?
Vonkaff.	Baltimore.	" —1823
Robinson, Albert.	?	? — ?
Taylor, William.	?	? —1821
Reyburn, James.	?	1821—1824
Price, Thomas.	?	" —1823
Schmidt, W.	?	" — "
Hoffman, William.	?	? —1824
Seghers, P., A. B.	Brussels.	? —1821
Carrere, August.	?	1822—1825
Chanche, J.	?	" —1826
Ducatel, A.	?	" —1820
Leloup, A., A. M.	Baltimore.	" —1828
Jenkins, A.	"	" —1825
Donalson, A., A. B.	"	? —1822
West, B., A. B.	"	? — "
Pinkney, T., A. M.	"	? — "
Tiernan, William, A. M.	"	? — "
Shriver, J. A., A. M.	?	1822—1827
Long, Robert.	?	" —1826
Baily, B.	?	" —1822
Schmidt, A.	Baltimore.	? — ?
Cockrane, J.	?	? —1822
Cockrane, E.	?	? — "
Hays, Benjamin, A. M.	?	1822—1827
Gegan, Joseph, A. M.	Ireland.	? —1822
Mickle, Edward.	Baltimore.	1822—1824

NAME.	RESIDENCE.	ENTRY AND DEPARTURE.
SCHROEDER, F.	?	? — ?
VENANT, J.	?	? —1823
McDOWELL, GEORGE.	?	1822—1824
HOWARD, H.	?	? — ?
PURVIANCE, W.	?	1822—1829
McMECHEN, C.	?	" —1824
LUCAS, J.	?	? —1822
DOIZE.	Baltimore.	1822—1825
NEMINGER, B.	"	? —1822
NEMINGER, J.	"	1822—1826
EGERTON, BENNET.	"	" —1829
HEWITT, E.	?	? — ?
CAVEDO.	?	1822—1822
CORTES, J.	?	" — "
BUCHANON, SMITH.	Baltimore.	" —1827
VICKERS, G.	?	" —1826
BRADFORD, AUG.	Maryland.	" —1824
DE NEURILLE.	?	" —1822
MARSHALL, W.	?	" — ?
FAIRBURN, J.	Baltimore.	1822—1826
BARRY, J.	"	" — "
OGDEN, JOHN, A. B.	"	" —1827
MYERS, A., A. B.	Pennsylvania.	" — "
HODGES, B.	?	" — "
EDMONDSON.	?	" — "
TIERNAN, M.	?	" —1829
GASTON, A., A. B.	North Carolina.	1823—1823
GREGAN, JAMES.	?	" —1827
KELLY, D.	Baltimore.	" — "
KELLY, P.	"	" — "
PLATA, S.	?	" —1826
WILLIAMSON, A.	?	" —1824
WHITE, A.	?	" —1827
DANIELS, JOHN.	?	" —1826
WALSH, ROBERT M.	Philadelphia.	" — "
BRYAN, THOMAS.	?	" —1828

NAME.	RESIDENCE.	ENTRY AND DEPARTURE.
Robinson, W.	?	1823—1826
Stinson, William.	?	" — ?
Meredith, T. T., A. M.	?	? —1823
McLaughlin, James.	Baltimore.	1823—1824
McLaughlin, B.	"	" — "
Purviance, James.	?	" —1823
Levering, Maris.	Baltimore.	" — "
Hindes, S.	"	" —1825
Myers, G.	?	" —1823
Williams, Thomas.	?	" —1826
Baker, William.	Baltimore.	" —1825
McBlair, P.	"	" —1824
McBlair, H.	"	" —1825
Rodman.	?	" —1823
Fairbairn, B.	?	" —1826
Blair, Henry.	Baltimore.	" — "
Barry, Thomas.	?	" — ?
Barry, David.	?	" —1824
Brand, Charles.	Baltimore.	" —1825
Mayer, Brantz.	?	" —1824
Freily, Thomas.	Baltimore.	" —1826
Krebs, E.	?	" — "
Turnbull, H.	Baltimore.	" —1825
Krumshaar, Alexander.	?	" — "
Gross, Jacob.	?	" — "
Hoffman, A.	?	" — "
Robinson, William.	?	" —1823
Mudd, Th.	Maryland.	" —1824
Barry, G.	?	" —1826
Edwards, William.	?	" —1823
Marsh, N.	Maryland.	" —1824
Stinson, William.	?	" —1823
McKim, H.	?	" — ?
Jado, F.	?	" —1826
Jado, Eml.	?	" — "
Barnum, A.	Baltimore.	" —1825
Wells, Henry.	?	" —1824

NAME.	RESIDENCE.	ENTRY AND DEPARTURE.
Carr, John.	?	1823—1824
Peterkin, W.	?	" — "
Keerl, W.	?	" — "
McKim, H.	?	" —1827
Chatard, F., A. B.	Baltimore.	? —1824
Mud, A., A. B.	Maryland.	? — "
Price, John.	?	1824—1825
McLaughlin, B.	Baltimore.	" —1827
McLaughlin, Thomas.	?	" —1828
Reyburn, James.	?	" —1825
Barry, D.	?	" —1827
Baltzell, C.	Baltimore.	" —1825
Mayer, B.	"	" — ?
Santana, C.	Caraccas.	" —1829
Santana, M.	"	" —1828
Troanas, R.	"	" —1827
Mullekin, R.	?	" —1829
Mullekin, E.	Baltimore.	" —1828
Hoskins, J.	?	" —1827
Hunter, John.	Baltimore.	" —1829
Gooding, John.	?	" —1825
Gooding, James.	?	" — "
Gooding, L.	?	" — "
Gooding, William.	?	" — "
Dawskins, W.	?	" —1826
Baker, James.	Baltimore.	" — "
Higgins, Francis.	?	" —1825
Ruffin, William K.	North Carolina.	" —1827
Jenkins, C.	?	" —1826
Scotti, E.	?	" —1825
Mazero, M.	?	" — ?
Santarem, Joseph.	Brazil.	" —1826
Schultz.	?	" —1824
Norris, Charles.	?	" — "
Smith, C.	?	" — "
Gould, A.	?	" —1827
Adams, A.	?	" —1825

NAME.	RESIDENCE.	ENTRY AND DEPARTURE.
Alexander, G.	?	1824—1825
Dumbar, William.	?	" — "
Millikin, R.	?	" —1824
Millikin, E.	?	" — "
Ward, P.	?	" — "
Martin, W. R.	?	" —1827
Bernabeu, John.	?	" —1825
Sims, Richard.	?	" — "
Morsell.	?	" — "
Dall, James.	?	" — "
Baker, G. W., A. B.	Baltimore.	" —1828
Dumbar, William.	?	" —1825
Shroeder, Francis.	Baltimore.	" — "
Hall, W.	?	" — "
McKim, John.	?	" —1829
Blair, W.	?	" —1827
Servary, J.	?	" — ?
Alexander, A.	?	" —1825
Riggs, S.	?	" — "
Williamson, A.	?	" — "
Brown, W.	?	" —1828
Spurrier.	Baltimore.	" — "
Dobbin, Robert.	?	" — "
Cugle, John.	?	" — "
Finley, R.	?	" —1827
Reip, A. H.	?	" —1826
Grey, Robert.	?	" —1825
Jenkins, James.	Baltimore.	" — "
Bodman, Philip.	?	" — "
Porter, A.	?	" — "
Neminger, B.	?	" — "
Dobbin, G.	?	" —1826
Bradford, A. W.	Hartford.	" —1824
Jenkins, O. L., A. M.	Baltimore.	1825—1831
Doisé, Henry.	"	" —1825
Bryan, Joseph.	"	" —1828
Farres, Joseph.	Havana.	" — "

NAME.	RESIDENCE.	ENTRY AND DEPARTURE.
Diaz, M.	Havana.	1825—1828
Marchand, A.	?	" —1825
Taylor, T.	Norfolk, Va.	" —1826
Barnum, A.	?	" — "
Aguires, A.	?	" — ?
Sierra, A.	Havana.	" —1828
Moussier, G.	New Orleans.	" —1827
Paez, Th.	?	" —1826
Paez, M.	?	" — "
Learet, P.	Havana.	" —1828
Caduc, P.	?	" — ?
Walsh, J.	?	" —1826
Trabuc.	?	" —1825
De Mareuil, Joseph.	?	" —1827
Iturbide, Angelo.	Mexico.	" — ?
Poe, G.	Pittsburg.	" —1827
Mazero, N.	Caraccas.	? — ?
Knight, E., A. M.	Baltimore.	? —1825
White, Charles, A. M.	"	? — "
William, William, A. B.	"	? — "
Stevenson, W., A. B.	"	? — "
Harris, B.	?	1825— "
Kempton, William.		" —1826
Beyburn, J.	Baltimore.	" — "
Vickery, G.	?	" — ?
Chayton, G.	?	" —1828
Chayton, E.	?	" — "
Aitken, L.	?	" — "
Webb, George.	Baltimore.	" —1827
Weeks, William.	?	" —1825
Purviance, G., A. M.	?	" —1833
Baltzel, C., A. M.	?	" — "
Mayer, B.	?	" —1826
Carrere, A.	?	" — "
Doisé.	?	" —1828
Williams, L.	Baltimore.	" —1829
Glenn, W.	?	" —1829

NAME.	RESIDENCE.	ENTRY AND DEPARTURE.
Shultz, H.	?	1825—1825
Smith, C.	?	" — "
Ward, Peregrine.	?	" — "
Reiniker.	Baltimore.	" —1829
Dorsey, Thomas.	?	" —1826
Renshan, R.	?	" —1825
Carns, John.	?	" —1826
Weeks.	?	" — "
Hammond, R.	?	" — "
Robinson, William.	Baltimore.	" — ?
Martin, John.	"	" — ?
Martin, Joseph.	"	" — ?
Bealmear, Thomas.	?	" —1827
Dall, James.	Baltimore.	" — ?
Boguier, Dk.	?	" —1827
Generes, L.	?	" —1829
Durham.	?	" —1827
Williams, John.	?	" —1828
Adams, Em.	?	" —1829
Dobbin, John.	Baltimore.	? — ?
Hall, Edward.	?	1825—1827
Walter, Fs.	?	" — "
Walter, C.	?	" —1828
Dobbin, George.	?	" —1826
Morales, N.	Bogota.	1826—1828
Cañedo, C.	Mexico.	" — "
Cañedo, V.	"	" — "
Mareuil, Joseph.	France.	" — ?
Jenkins, Joseph.	Baltimore.	" —1827
Hilden, Sal.	?	? — ?
Lusby, William.	Baltimore.	1826—1827
Cormick, L., A. B.	Augusta.	" —1830
Jenkins, M. C., A. B.	Baltimore.	? —1826
Woods, G.	"	1826—1829
Walter, Francis.	?	? — ?
Van Bibber, Charles.	Philadelphia.	1826—1826
Van Bibber, James.	"	" — "

STUDENTS OF ST. MARY'S COLLEGE.

NAME.	RESIDENCE.	ENTRY AND DEPARTURE.
COLE, WILLIAM.	Baltimore.	1826—1827
GOLD, P.	"	" —1828
GOLD, G.	"	" — "
GOLD, L.	"	" — "
GOLD, JOSEPH.	"	" — "
FENNER, B.	?	" —1826
GOODWIN, JOHN.	?	" — "
GOODWIN, WILLIAM.	?	" —1828
GOODWIN, L.	?	" — "
GOODWIN, FREDERICK.	?	" — "
CLAGETT, WILLIAM.	Baltimore.	" — ?
WADDELL, JAMES.	?	" —1827
HAILY.	Baltimore.	" —1829
CORY, BENJAMIN.	?	" —1827
MONMONIER, J.	"	" — ?
DALL, JAMES.	"	" —1829
BOQUIER, D.	?	1827— ?
TESSON, E.	Missouri.	" —1829
ALSUA, B.	?	" — ?
ALSUA, M.	Quanquill.	" — ?
SANTANA, JOSEPH.	Caracas.	" — ?
SOCARA, F.	?	" —1828
NOŸ, F.	Puerto de Principe.	" — "
WALSH, JOSEPH.	Philadelphia.	" — "
OGDEN, J.	Baltimore.	? — ?
SCHROEDER, H. A., A. B.	"	? —1827
WHITE, A. A., A. B.	"	? — "
HOSKINS, J. H., A. M.	"	? — "
LEARY, C.	?	" —1828
HAYDEN, EDWIN.	?	" — ?
NEMINGER, JOHN.	Baltimore.	" —1827
FLEETWOOD, STANLEY.	"	" —1829
SPURRIER, GD.	Louisiana.	" —1828
CLONEY.	?	" —1827
CHAISTY, EDWARD.	Baltimore.	" —1829
ROBINSON, J.	"	" — ?
ROBINSON, C.	"	" — ?

NAME.	RESIDENCE.	ENTRY AND DEPARTURE.
Kracht, Edward.	Baltimore.	1827—1829
Inloes, Henry A., A. B.	"	" — "
Buckler, Thomas.	?	" — "
Denison, Robert M.	Baltimore.	" — ?
Dumington, A.	"	" — ?
Dumington, F.	"	" — ?
Ewalt, Augustus.	?	" —1829
Hazlehurst, Andrew.	?	" —1828
Hazlehurst, Samuel.	?	" — "
Servari, J.	Baltimore.	" —1829
Seeds, J. L.	"	" — ?
Sommerville, William.	"	" — ?
Skinner, Theodore.	?	" —1829
Slingluf.	?	" — "
Smith, Samuel.	?	" —1828
Williamson, D.	Baltimore.	" —1829
Musl, Joseph, A. M.	Maryland.	" —1828
Harris, Joseph.	?	" —1829
Poultney, B.	?	" — ?
McLaughlin, D.	?	1828—1829
Trwin, William.	Alexandria.	" —1828
Tyson, A.	?	" — "
Leakin, William.	?	" —1829
McIntosh, J.	Martinique.	" —1833
Biddle, John B., A. M.	Philadelphia.	" —1832
Baily, A.	Maryland.	" —1830
Robinson, Joseph.	Baltimore.	" —1833
Hunter, Thomas.	?	" —1829
Shiff, Edward.	?	" —1830
Maspero, P.	New Orleans.	" —1833
McLane, Robert.	?	" — "
Bryan, M. F., A. B.	Georgia.	" —1828
Elder, Joseph.	Baltimore.	" — "
Elder, Thomas.	"	" —1831
Palmer, William.	?	" —1829
Owens, B.	Baltimore.	" —1830
Wallis, P.	"	" —1832

Most Rev. Samuel Eccleston, D. D.,
Fifth Archbishop of Baltimore.

STUDENTS OF ST. MARY'S COLLEGE.

NAME.	RESIDENCE.	ENTRY AND DEPARTURE.
WALLIS, S. T., L. L. D.	Baltimore.	1828—1832
STANARD, G.	"	" — ?
PURVIANCE, G., A. M.	"	" —1833
BOQUIER, D.	?	" —1829
BROWN, WILLIAM.	?	" —1828
BYRNE, THOS.	?	" —1834
COLVIN, H.	?	" —1828
FARRES, JOSEPH.	?	" — "
GROVERMAN, CHARLES.	?	" —1829
HARRIS, HENRY.	?	" — "
HUSSEY, JOSEPH.	?	" — "
PIPER, CHARLES.	?	" — "
PALMER, JOSEPH.	?	" — "
SALMON, EDWARD.	?	" —1832
SALMON, CHARLES.	?	" — "
TYSON, A.	?	" —1829
MCLAUGHLIN, M.	?	" — "
WINN, N.	?	" — "
DALRYMPLE, JOHN.	Baltimore.	" —1834
DORNEY, JOHN.	?	" —1829
FRAILY, G.	?	" — "
FRAILY, P.	?	" — ?
WEVER, JOHN.	?	" —1829
MCLEANE, JOHN.	?	" —1833
GOODWIN, JOHN.	?	" —1829
GOODWIN, THOMAS.	?	" — "
CAUSTIN, J.	?	" —1829
WEBB, G.	?	1829— ?
BALTZELL, C., A. B.	Baltimore.	" —1833
RAMON, JOSE.	Menchaca.	" — ?
WALSH, JOSEPH.	?	" —1829
CHATARD, JOSEPH.	Baltimore.	" —1833
MCLAUGHLIN, JOHN.	?	" —1832
AROSEMENA, PAUL.	Columbia.	" —1834
AROSEMENA, JAMES.	"	" — "
PHILIPPS, PHILIP.	New Orleans.	" — ?
BARCLAY, JOHN O., A. M.	Philadelphia.	" —1833

NAME.	RESIDENCE.	ENTRY AND DEPARTURE.
Turull, Joseph.	?	1829— ?
Guerrero, Joseph.	Porto Rico.	" — ?
Muncks, John.	Baltimore.	" — ?
Chaisty, Edward, A. M.	Baltimore.	" —1832
Marie, P.	?	" —1833
Potter, Z. W.	Maryland.	" — "
Purviance, W. H.	Baltimore.	? —1829
Stewart, A.	"	1829— "
Stewart, C.	"	" — "
Claxton, F.	"	" —1834
Doyle, John.	Chicago.	" —1829
Zell, Charles.	?	" — "
De Ronserey.	Baltimore.	" — "
Arosemana, Pablo.	Columbia.	" — "
Arosemana, Diego.	"	" — "
Lea, Isaac.	?	" —1830
Randall, J.	Baltimore.	" —1832
Frazier, J.	"	" —1830
Gallagher, Eph.	?	" —1829
Muse, James.	?	" —1830
Armstrong, John.	?	" —1830
Armsted, Henry.	Baltimore.	" —1830
Boarman, Charles.	?	" — ?
Cole, James.	?	" —1832
Hickman, Wm. H.	Baltimore.	" — "
Handy, Jesse.	?	" —1830
Klockengether, Edward.	Baltimore.	" —1836
Leary, Cornelius.	?	" —1831
Leakin, Wm.	?	" —1830
Myers, A.	?	" —1833
Nenninger, M.	Baltimore.	" — "
Poor, Elliot J.	"	" — "
Rony.	?	" — ?
Ripoll, Joseph.	?	" —1830
Walter, C.	?	" —1832
Williams, Henry.	?	" —1833
Coskrey, Joseph.	Baltimore.	" —1834

STUDENTS OF ST. MARY'S COLLEGE. 115

NAME.	RESIDENCE.	ENTRY AND DEPARTURE.
POWER, W.	Baltimore.	1829—1833
GROVERNA.	?	" —1829
SALMON, E.	Baltimore.	" —1832
SALMON, C.	"	" — "
DERONARY, TH.	?	" —1833
HEALY, MICHAEL.	Baltimore.	" —1832
MITCHELL, JOSEPH.	Maryland.	" —1834
REISIG, FREDERICK.	Buenos Ayres.	" — "
BARRY, DAVID.	Baltimore.	1830—1832
BARRY, JAMES.	"	" — "
BARRY, CARL.	"	" — "
BARRY, WILLIAM.	"	" — "
GOLL, JAMES.	"	" — ?
BANDNY, PETER.	?	" — ?
BANKHEAD, JAMES.	?	" —1833
BROOMWELL, JOHN.	?	" — "
JACKSON, JOSEPH.	?	" — ?
MURPHY, P.	Ireland.	" — ?
COLE, GEORGE W.	?	" —1832
CARRIERE, VICTOR.	?	" — ?
CONY, BENJAMIN.	?	" — ?
DESHEILL, RICHARD.	?	" — ?
DALACOSTA, ANTONIO.	Caraccas.	" —1834
DALACOSTA, JOHN BAPTIST.	"	" —1832
GALL, JOSEPH.	?	" — ?
GRATZ, HYMEN.	?	" — ?
GAUDSY, AMAND A.	?	" — ?
HOFFMAN, FREDERICK W.	?	" — ?
ALPHONSO, JOSEPH.	?	" — ?
BASSORA, MANUEL.	?	" — ?
HICKWICK, CHARLES.	?	1831— ?
HICKWICK, FR.	?	" — ?
MESTRE, C. P.	?	1831— ?
HODGES, CHARLES.	?	1830— ?
KELLY, MATH.	Baltimore.	" —1833
KELLER, ALEXANDER, A. M.	Alabama.	" —1832
LA REINTRIE, H.	Baltimore.	" — ?

NAME.	RESIDENCE.	ENTRY AND DEPARTURE.
LUKE, W.	?	1830— ?
NUNCHACA, R.	?	" — ?
LAROQUE, ALEXIS.	Baltimore.	" —1834
DENISON, R. M., A. B.	"	" —1830
DUNCAN, HH.	?	" —1832
NEGRETE, JOSEPH.	?	" — "
BERGART, HENRY.	?	" — "
REPPERT, JACOB.	Baltimore.	" —1833
READ, S. P.	South Carolina.	" — "
STENSON, FENWICK.	Baltimore.	" — "
SMITH, SAMUEL.	?	" —1832
SPENCE, ROBERT.	Baltimore.	" —1835
FERRO, JOHN AND ANT.	?	" —1833
TAYLOR, J.	?	" — "
THOMPSON, JOHN.	?	" —1834
WILLIAMSON, ADOLPHE.	Baltimore.	" — "
WEIGH, HENRY.	?	" —1832
WIGH, OLIVER.	?	" — "
YTURBIDE, SALVADOR.	Mexico.	1831— "
ACKLAND, JOHN.	Baltimore.	" —1833
BADEN, JAMES.	"	" —1834
BOGG, WILLIAM.	?	" — "
BAKER, HENRY.	?	" — "
BANGHMAN, FRAN.	?	" —1833
BEVANS, CHARLES.	?	" — "
BIXLER, LEWIS.	?	" — "
BIXLER, M.	?	" — "
BAILEY, GEORGE.	?	" —1832
BACON, JAMES.	?	" —1833
BRADFORD.	?	" — "
CARRIERE, VICTOR.	?	" — ?
DE CHOISEUL, CHARLES.	?	" — ?
CHAPPELL, W.	?	" —1831
DALLAM, H.	?	" — "
FOLEY, D.	Baltimore.	" —1834
DOWLING, THOMAS.	"	? — ?
RUBIO, M.	Mexico.	1831—1833

STUDENTS OF ST. MARY'S COLLEGE. 117

NAME.	RESIDENCE.	ENTRY AND DEPARTURE.
RUBIO, JOSE.	Mexico.	1831—1833
GIRANDY, ANGELO.	?	" — ?
NUIBY, F.	?	" — ?
VINCENT, ANTONIO.	Cuba.	" —1833
MILLS, WILLIAM.	Baltimore.	" — "
BORIL.	?	" — ?
DONALSON.	?	" —1833
FORSTER.	?	" — ?
FEAST, WILLIAM.	Baltimore.	" —1833
FLINT, HENRY.	?	" —1834
FLINT, R.	?	" — "
STEVENSON, G. P.	Baltimore.	" —1833
HERRON, ALEXANDER.	?	" — ?
HOLMES.	?	" — ?
HOWARD, JOHN.	?	" — ?
HITSELBERGER, FRANCIS.	Baltimore.	" —1833
HAYS, JOSEPH.	?	" —1834
COCKARILL, JOHN.	Virginia.	" —1833
HARDING, W. H.	"	" — "
JAMISON, W. D.	?	" — "
JAMISON.	?	" — "
KING, FRANCIS.	Baltimore.	" —1834
KIERL, HENRY.	?	" — ?
KIERL, THOMAS.	?	" — ?
KING, THOMAS.	Baltimore.	" —1834
KALKMAN.	?	" —1832
LAFITTE, CH.	Baltimore.	" —1834
LAFITTE, H.	"	" —1833
LA REINTRIE, LOUIS.	"	" — "
LAWVENSON, F.	?	" — "
MAGUIRE, THOMAS.	?	" — "
RAMSAY, MCHENRY.	Baltimore.	" —1832
RAMSAY, JOSEPH.	?	" — "
STUMP, ALEXANDER H.	?	" — ?
SUMNER, JOHN.	Baltimore.	" —1833
SINNOTT, JOHN.	"	" — "
TORNELL, JOSE M.	?	" — ?

NAME.	RESIDENCE.	ENTRY AND DEPARTURE.
TORNELL, AUGUSTUS.	?	1831— ?
TORNELL, MANUEL.	?	" — ?
WALTER, F.	Baltimore.	" —1832
WALTER, CH.	"	" — "
HUELIN, MATHIAS.	Malaga.	1832—1834
HUELIN, WILLIAM.	"	" —1837
MITCHELL, JOSEPH.	Baltimore.	" —1834
LEVERING, ALEXANDER.	"	" — "
LEVERING, CHARLES.	"	" —1839
MCENERY, DONAT.	"	" —1834
MOREAU, OSCAR.	New Orleans.	" —1839
ROUSSEAU, JAMES.	Cuba.	" —1837
MOORE, NATHAN.	?	" —1833
MERCER, JOHN F.	Maryland.	" —1834
MILLER, JAMES WILLIAM, A. B.	New Orleans.	" —1837
NORRIS, RICHARD.	?	" —1833
PARR, JAMES.	Baltimore.	" —1834
POOR, J. H.	"	" — "
ROBINSON, J. WASH.	?	" —1833
ROGERS, G. H.	?	" — "
SLINGLUFF, UPTON.	Baltimore.	" —1834
SHANE.	?	" —1833
SPENSE, CARROLL.	Baltimore.	" —1834
SPENSE, CHARLES.	"	" — "
SMITH, B.	?	" — "
SMITH, LAMBERT.	Baltimore.	" — "
TILGMAN.	?	" — ?
GEORGE.	?	" — ?
WATTLES.	?	" —1833
WALKERS, ALEXANDER.	?	" —1834
WATTER, GEORGE.	Baltimore.	" — "
NELSON, WILLIAM.	Maryland.	" — "
BYRNE, J., A. M.	Baltimore.	" —1835
BOGGS, W. A., A. B.	"	" —1834
BOGGS, JAMES.	"	" —1837
CAIN, WILLIAM.	"	" —1834
CLENDINEN, W.	"	" — "

NAME.	RESIDENCE.	ENTRY AND DEPARTURE.
NELSON, H. C., A. M.	Baltimore.	1832—1838
CLAGET, OTHO.	"	" —1834
CLAGET, ELY.	"	" — "
CLAGET, EDWARD.	"	" — "
CORBELL, HENRY.	North Carolina.	" — "
GIRAUDI, L.	Cuba.	" — "
DRAYTON, W. H., A. M.	Charleston, S. C.	? —1833
GREEN.	?	1832— "
HAYS, B.	Baltimore.	" —1834
HUGHES, J.	?	" — ?
HAMILTON, THOMAS.	?	" —1834
LAUVE, ULGER.	New Orleans.	" — "
DAVID, JULIUS.	?	" — ?
HEALD, JOHN.	Baltimore.	" —1834
HARRISON, BENJAMIN.	"	" — "
HARRISON, THOMAS.	"	" — "
PUBLIERO, LOUIS.	?	" —1833
AMADOR, EPHEMIUS.	Mexico.	1833— ?
ARMITAGE, JAMES.	Baltimore.	" — ?
BACON, JAMES.	"	" — ?
BASORA, JOHN.	Porto Rico.	" —1834
BLANCO, RICHARD.	Cuba.	" — "
BLANCO, URBAN.	"	" — "
CANOVAS, MANUEL.	Mexico.	" —1838
CLAXTON, ALEXANDER.	Baltimore.	" — ?
CHRISTHILF, GEORGE.	"	" — ?
DALLA COSTA, JOHN.	Angostura.	" —1836
DALLA COSTA, CESAR.	"	" — "
HARDING, THOMAS.	Virginia.	" —1834
HEALD, EDWARD.	Baltimore.	" — ?
HEDRICKS, ROBERT.	"	" —1834
HODGES, THOMAS HARRIS.	"	" — "
HOOK, DANIEL.	"	" —1838
KING, THOMAS.	"	" — ?
KIRKLAND, WILLIAM.	"	" —1838
LUCAS, HENRY.	"	" —1840
MANGUAL, RAPHAEL.	Porto Rico.	1834—1835

NAME.	RESIDENCE.	ENTRY AND DEPARTURE.
MANGUAL, CHARLES.	Porto Rico.	1833—1835
MILES, GEORGE H.	Baltimore.	" — ?
MUNCKS, ANDREW.	"	" —1839
MCMURTRIE, JAMES.	Philadelphia.	" — "
MCMURTRIE, FRANCIS.	"	" —1836
MONTGOMERY, AUGUSTUS.	New Orleans.	" —1835
NEAL, JAMES.	Baltimore.	" — ?
NICHOLSON, JAMES.	New Orleans.	" —1841
NICHOLSON, JOHN.	" "	" — "
NUIRY, FREDERICK L.	Cuba.	" —1839
O'FARRELL, FRANCIS.	Baltimore.	" — ?
PLANO, ANGELO.	Cuba.	" —1838
PLANO, AUGUSTIN.	"	" —1839
PUÑAN, JOSEPH D.	Porto Rico.	" — ?
ROUSSEAU, ALFRED.	New Orleans.	" — ?
RUSSELL, THOMAS.	Savannah.	" —1835
SANS, FRANCIS.	Malaga.	" —1838
SEARS, WILLIAM.	Baltimore.	" — ?
SERVARY, GEORGE.	"	" —1838
SHRIVER, ALFRED.	"	" —1834
VINCENT, JAMES.	Cuba.	" —1838
WALDBURG, GEORGE M.	Savannah.	" —1834
WINTER, HENRY.	Baltimore.	" — ?
WINTER, CHARLES.	"	" — ?
ADAMS, BUSHROD WASHINGTON.	Philadelphia.	" —1836
ALPHONSO, JOSEPH B.	Porto Rico.	" —1835
ARCAMBAL, CHARLES.	Baltimore.	" — "
BADEN, BENJAMIN.	"	" — "
BASORA, MANUEL J.	Porto Rico.	" — ?
BOEHM, EDWARD.	Baltimore.	" —1835
BOWER, JACOB.	"	" — ?
BRADFORD, GEORGE.	"	" — ?
CASADO, DOMINGO.	Malaga.	" — ?
CHABOT, LAWRENCE, M. D.	Baltimore.	" — ?
CLAXTON, FRANCIS.	"	" —1838
CRAIG, WHARTON.	Philadelphia.	" —1836
DALL, JOSEPH.	Baltimore.	" — ?

STUDENTS OF ST. MARY'S COLLEGE.

NAME.	RESIDENCE.	ENTRY AND DEPARTURE.
Dalla Costa, Antony.	Angostura.	1833—1839
Dowling, Thomas, P.	Baltimore.	" — ?
Elizondo, Jerome.	Caraccas.	" —1838
Elmore, Lewis W.	Baltimore.	" — ?
Foley, Thomas.	"	" —1841
Heron, James.	"	" —1834
Hill, Charles, A. B.	Maryland.	" —1838
Huelin, William.	Malaga.	" — "
Laws, John.	Baltimore.	" — ?
Little, Henry.	"	" — ?
McLane, Louis.	Delaware.	" —1834
Nenninger, Frederick.	Baltimore.	" — "
Pearson, John.	"	" —1836
Reip, Edward.	"	" —1834
Reissig, Frederick.	Buenos Ayres.	" — ?
Stenson, Fenwick J.	Baltimore.	" —1836
Spurrier, Rudolph.	"	" —1838
Spurrier, Jay.	"	" — "
Stokes, Robert.	"	" — ?
Wickersham, John.	"	" —1835
West, Hilborne.	Philadelphia.	" —1834
Barney, Samuel Chase.	Baltimore.	" — ?
Blenkinsop, William, A. M.	"	" —1839
Dall, Austin.	"	" —1834
Gittings, Rumsey.	"	" — ?
Healy, Patrick.	"	" —1834
La Reintrie, Henry.	"	" — "
Lucas, William F.	"	" — ?
Maguire, Joseph, A. M.	"	" —1838
Ogden, Bananiel.	"	" — ?
Pearson, George.	"	" — ?
Richards, Stephen.	"	" —1834
Smith, Dennis, A. M.	"	" —1838
Tubman, George H.	Maryland.	" —1836
Williams, Otho H.	Baltimore.	" —1838
Baker, William J.	North Carolina.	" —1835
Bruce, Charles.	Baltimore.	" — ?

NAME.	RESIDENCE.	ENTRY AND DEPARTURE.
COMBS, LEWIS C.	Maryland.	1833—1836
CARROLL, DAVID W.	Baltimore.	" —1834
DANELS, JAMES.	"	" — ?
DIGGES, CHARLES.	Washington, D. C.	" —1834
ELDER, EDWARD, A. M.	Maryland.	" —1836
FORMAN, WILLIAM.	Baltimore.	" — ?
GUNN, JOHN P., M. D.	"	" — ?
HODGES, CHARLES.	"	" — ?
IZARD, R. DELANCEY.	Philadelphia.	" — ?
LAROQUE, ALEXIS.	Baltimore.	" —1834
LEWIS, STOCKER, A. M.	Philadelphia.	" —1837
MUNCKS, JOHN.	Baltimore.	" —1834
PLANO, PAUL.	Cuba.	" — "
ROCKHILL, ABRAHAM.	Philadelphia.	" — "
SPURRIER, WINDHAM.	Baltimore.	" — "
THOMPSON, JOHN.	"	" — ?
VINENT, ANTONIO.	Cuba.	" —1834
WHELAN, GEORGE J.	Baltimore.	" —1836
BLENKINSOP, PETER, S. J.	"	" — ?
CHATARD, JOSEPH.	"	" —1834
COAD, GEORGE, A. M.	Maryland.	" —1836
COMBS, PHILIP, A. M.	"	" —1834
DALRYMPLE, JOHN.	Baltimore.	" — ?
LEMMON, WILLIAM.	"	" — ?
MERRICK, WILLIAM.	Maryland.	" —1834
MITCHELL, JOSEPH T.	Baltimore.	" — ?
MONTGOMERY, RICHARD.	New Orleans.	" —1835
MONTGOMERY, WILLIAM H.	" "	" — ?
NEILSON, JAMES C.	Baltimore.	" — ?
ROCKHILL, THOMAS C., A. M.	Philadelphia.	" —1836
SPENCE, CARROLL.	Baltimore.	" — ?
THOMAS, WILLIAM H., A. M.	Maryland.	" —1836
WILLIAMS, WILLIAM S.	Baltimore.	" — ?
WINCHESTER, JOHN M.	"	" —1835
BARRY, WILLIAM J.	"	" —1835
BROMWELL, HOSEA J.	"	" — ?
BURTON, JOHN F.	North Carolina.	" — ?

NAME.	RESIDENCE.	ENTRY AND DEPARTURE.
Danels, Lewis D.	Baltimore.	1833—1834
Graham, Richard.	Washington, D. C.	" — ?
McCulloch, Hezekiah.	Baltimore.	" — ?
Peters, Francis.	Philadelphia.	" —1834
Perkins, Jonathan.	Connecticut.	" — ?
Ridgely, Henry M., A. M.	Delaware.	" —1836
Barry, Garrett, A. M.	Baltimore.	" —1835
Bauduy, Peter.	Philadelphia.	" — ?
Biddle, George W., A. M.	"	" —1835
Horwitz, Orville, A. M.	Baltimore.	" — ?
Poultney, Benjamin, A. M.	"	" —1834
West, James, A. M.	Philadelphia.	" —1835
Coskrey, H. B., A. M.	?	" —1834
Baltzell, Columbus, A. B.	Baltimore.	" — ?
Waggaman, H. J.	?	" — ?
Nelson, John L.	Baltimore.	1834—1838
Arcambal, Francis.	"	" —1836
Nelson, Roger.	Maryland.	" — "
Poor, John H.	Baltimore.	" — "
Sanches, Joseph.	Malaga.	" — "
Bennett, William J.	Baltimore.	" — "
Boggs, James.	"	" — "
Dall, Joseph.	?	1833—1834
Aiken, Robert.	?	1835—1841
Byrne, Kavin.	?	1834—1834
Mills, William.	?	" — "
Dashields, N. L.	Baltimore.	" — ?
Fisher, George.	?	" —1835
Giraudi, A.	?	" —1836
Green, Stephen.	?	" — "
Green, Isaiah.	?	" — "
Gold, Charles.	?	1835— "
Heerman, Ad. Th.	?	1834—1835
Heerman, Valentine.	?	" — "
Horton, E. Tudor.	Baltimore.	" —1836
Howel, Ralph Higinbottom.	?	1835— "
Lawrence, Stocker.	Baltimore.	1834—1834

NAME.	RESIDENCE.	ENTRY AND DEPARTURE.
WALLACE, THOMAS.	?	1834—1835
McCOLGAN, EDWARD J.	?	" —1836
McCANN, FERDINAND.	?	" —1835
MOALE, HENRY.	Baltimore.	" —1840
McLANE, ALLAN.	"	" —1840
McLANE, GEORGE.	"	" — "
PERKINS, E.	?	" —1835
POOR, ELLIOTT.	Baltimore.	" — ?
POTTER, ZEBDIEL.	?	" —1835
RICHARDS, GEORGE.	?	" —1836
REYBURN, JOHN.	Baltimore.	" — ?
AIKEN, ROBERT.	?	1835—1841
CARROLL, HENRY J.	Maryland.	" —1836
DUKEHART.	?	" — "
HALL E.	New Orleans.	" — "
HICKMAN, GEORGE.	Baltimore.	" — "
MEALY.	?	" — "
OLDFIELD, GRANVILLE J.	Baltimore.	" —1837
POWELL, DEVAN BARING.	Philadelphia.	" —1836
POWELL, HARE.	"	" — "
ROENNE, JULIUS.	?	" — "
ARCHER, RICHARD.	?	1836— ?
BEACHAM, JAMES.	Baltimore.	" —1837
BRANDT, JAMES.	New Orleans.	" — "
CAGE, ALBERT G.	Mississippi.	" — "
CASAMAJOR, EDWARD.	San Jago de Cuba.	" —1838
CLIFTON, THEODORE.	Baltimore.	" —1840
CORRIGAN, HUGH.	"	" —1838
DE PESTRE, EDMUND.	Matanzas.	? — ?
DOMENECH, JOHN P.	"	1836—1837
DOMENECH, PHILIP.	"	" — "
FABRÉ, JOSEPH.	San Jago de Cuba.	" — "
FAHEY, JOHN.	Baltimore.	" —1840
GAMIZ, GENARO.	Mexico.	" —1837
GEDDES, JAMES.	Baltimore.	" — "
HURTUBISE, CHARLES V.	New Orleans.	" —1841
HURTUBISE, ALFRED.	" "	" —1840

STUDENTS OF ST. MARY'S COLLEGE.

NAME.	RESIDENCE.	ENTRY AND DEPARTURE.
JENKINS, JOHN.	Baltimore.	1836—1837
LAFITTE, JOHN.	"	" —1838
McLOSKEY, JAMES.	Mobile.	" —1839
McLOSKEY, JOHN.	"	" —1838
McPHERSON, JAMES.	Baltimore.	" —1837
MUNDER, CHARLES.	"	" — "
NAVARETTE, MANUEL.	Mexico.	" — "
OGDEN, AMBROSE.	Baltimore.	" —1839
PIERCE, WILLIAM.	New Orleans.	" —1838
PLOWMAN, JOHN A.	New York.	" —1839
POMIE, LUCIEN.	San Jago de Cuba.	" — ?
RINGOLD, WILLIAM.	Baltimore.	" —1837
SATLER, THOMAS C.	New York.	" —1838
SCOTT, HENRY.	Baltimore.	" —1840
SEWELL, RICHARD.	"	? — ?
SPILMAN, THOMAS.	"	1836—1839
STEWART, JOHN.	"	" —1838
STEWART, CHARLES.	"	" —1839
THOMAS, EDWIN.	"	" —1838
BOARMAN, THOMAS.	"	" —1837
CAGE, DUNCAN S.	Mississippi.	" — "
DELOSTE, JOSEPH.	Baltimore.	" —1838
ESMOND, BERNARD.	Maine.	" — "
EYRE, CALEB C.	Philadelphia.	" — ?
FIGANIERE, HENRY DE.	Lisbon.	" — ?
FRANCIS, FLEETWOOD.	Baltimore.	" — ?
GREENWAY, HENRY.	"	" — ?
GRISWOLD, DAVID.	Florida.	" — ?
GRISWOLD, CHARLES C.	"	" — ?
HALL, JAMES.	New Orleans.	" — ?
HART, FRANCIS.	Baltimore.	" —1838
HAYS, HENRY T.	Mississippi.	" —1837
HEWLETT, ANDREW.	Baltimore.	" — "
HUELIN, EDWARD.	Malaga.	" —1840
JOHNSON, REVERDY.	Baltimore.	" —1838
LAWN, JAMES.	"	" —1839
LESCAILLE, HENRY.	San Jago de Cuba.	" —1838

NAME.	RESIDENCE.	ENTRY AND DEPARTURE.
McCredy, Thomas, A. B.	Philadelphia.	1836—1842
Menzies, James.	Baltimore.	" —1837
Prevost, Aristides.	"	" —1838
Shields, Thomas.	New Orleans.	" —1839
Sprigg, Francis.	Baltimore.	" — "
Tilghman, Samuel.	"	? — ?
Thebaud, Edward P.	New York.	1836—1838
Walsh, Jasper.	Philadelphia.	" — "
Wallis, John.	Baltimore.	" — "
Wickersham, William.	"	1834— "
Whelan, Lewis.	"	1836— "
Woodville, Richard Caton.	"	" —1839
Armant, Terence.	New Orleans.	" —1838
Baltzell, William H., A. M.	Tennessee.	" —1841
Caravia, Joseph.	Montevideo.	" —1837
Cardeza, Joseph M., A. M.	Philadelphia.	" —1838
Charters, James B.	New York.	" — ?
Eitzen, Charles D.	Baltimore.	" — ?
Gosling, Henry.	Caracas.	" — ?
Gosling, William.	"	" — ?
Hammond, William M.	Maryland.	" — ?
Hill, John.	"	" — ?
Hughes, Edward.	Baltimore.	" —1837
Johnston, Christopher.	"	" — "
Lafitte, Henry B.	"	" — "
Nott, George.	New Orleans.	" —1841
Somerville, James.	Baltimore.	" — ?
Swan, John.	"	" —1839
Toledano, Julius.	New Orleans.	" — "
Walker, John M.	Baltimore.	" —1837
Walsh, Oliver.	Philadelphia.	" —1838
Whelan, Lewis.	Baltimore.	" —1837
Wilkins, Joseph.	"	" — "
Williams, James.	Maryland.	" — "
Domenech, Joseph M.	Matanzas.	" — "
Foley, Thomas, A. M.	Baltimore.	" —1840
Gibson, William, A. M.	"	" —1839

RT. REV. JOHN J. CHANCHE, D. D.,
Second Bishop of Natchez.

NAME.	RESIDENCE.	ENTRY AND DEPARTURE.
GLOVER, ROBERT O.	New York.	1836—1846
GORDON, GEORGE N., A. M.	North Carolina.	" —1840
GROSS, HENRY.	Baltimore.	" —1838
HUERGO, PALEMON.	Buenos Ayres.	" —1837
KEENAN, CHARLES, A. M.	Baltimore.	" —1840
KIRBY, JOHN H.	"	" —1838
LUSBY, CHARLES.	"	" — "
MALLOY, JOHN, A. M.	"	" —1840
SEMMES, IGNATIUS.	Maryland.	" —1838
SHRIVER, JOHN ALEXANDER.	Baltimore.	" —1837
SPRIGG, WILLIAM.	"	" —1839
WRIGHT, RIGNAL.	"	" — ?
CASTRO, BENITO.	Havana.	" —1837
GREENWAY, EDWARD.	Baltimore.	" — "
KEATING, WILLIAM V., A. M.	Philadelphia.	" —1840
MIER, JOACHIM.	Santa Martha.	" —1838
MARSHALL, JAMES.	Baltimore.	" — "
NORIEGA, MARCELINO.	Havana.	" — "
REARDON, BIRCKHEAD.	Baltimore.	" —1839
SHAEFER, ADOLPHUS C.	"	" —1838
TILGHMAN, JOHN C.	Maryland.	" — "
WILLIAMS, JOHN H.	"	" —1837
WILSON, JAMES.	Baltimore.	" — "
CARDEZA, JOHN T. M.	Philadelphia.	" —1838
HALL, ESMOND.	New Orleans.	" —1837
LEWIS, LAURENCE.	Philadelphia.	" — "
POWELL, WILLIAM.	North Carolina.	" — "
SPRIGG, JOSEPH.	Baltimore.	" —1838
DAVIS, PETER R., A. M.	North Carolina.	1836
HOOKE, RICHARD B., A. B.	Mississippi.	" —1837
HOOKE, MOSES J., A. B.	"	" — "
DEVEREUX, J. C., A. M.	Utica.	1836
BAER, WARREN.	New Orleans.	1837—1839
BENNETT, MATTHEW, A. B.	Baltimore.	1838—1844
CANONGE, DAWSON.	New Orleans.	" —1840
CANONGE, EDGAR.	" "	" —1839
CHACON, GEORGE.	Philadelphia.	" — "

NAME.	RESIDENCE.	ENTRY AND DEPARTURE
Chacon, Charles.	Philadelphia.	1838—1839
Chartrand, Philip.	Matanzas.	" — "
Chartrand, Augustus.	"	" — "
Danels, Bolivar, A. M.	Baltimore.	" —1844
Danels, Joseph.	"	" —1839
Durke, John.	"	" — "
Fabré, Joseph.	San Jago de Cuba.	" — "
Gamiz, Genero.	Mexico.	" —1842
Gregg, Andrew.	Baltimore.	" —1839
Hall, Francis X.	Maryland.	" — "
Hickley, Robert.	Baltimore.	" — "
Higginson, William.	"	" — "
Hooper, John.	"	" — "
Howard, William.	"	" — "
Ingraham, Duncan.	Philadelphia.	" — "
Jones, Edward.	Baltimore.	" — "
Madriz, Charles.	Caraccas.	" — "
Marsh, Samuel.	Philadelphia.	" — "
Massicott, Robert.	Baltimore.	" — "
McLane, George.	Delaware.	" — "
Menzies, Francis.	Baltimore.	" — "
Mullan, John.	"	" — "
Navarete, Manuel.	Mexico.	" — "
O'Keefe, David.	Baltimore.	" — "
Pomié, Lucien.	San Jago de Cuba.	" — ?
Prévost, Victor.	Baltimore.	" —1839
Riggs, Remus.	"	" — "
Ringgold, William.	"	" — "
Robertson, Zacharie.	New Orleans.	" — "
Smith, John W.	Baltimore.	" — "
Toole, John.	"	" — "
Walker, Charles.	"	" — "
Waters, James.	New Orleans.	" — "
Waters, Henry.	" "	" — "
Cage, Albert.	Mississippi.	" — "
Claxton, Alexander.	Baltimore.	" — "
Creny, William.	"	" — "

NAME.	RESIDENCE.	ENTRY AND DEPARTURE.
FIGANIERE, HENRY DE.	Lisbon.	1838—1839
HURTUBISE, ALFRED.	New Orleans.	" — "
JENKINS, FELIX.	Baltimore.	" — "
JOHNSTON, ELLIOT.	"	" — "
JOHNSTON, THOMAS.	"	" — "
MADRIZ, SIMON.	Caraccas.	" — "
MCFAUL, JAMES.	Baltimore.	" — "
MACKENZIE, GEORGE M.	"	" — "
MCWILLIAMS, PATRICK.	"	" — "
PARKER, OLIVER.	"	" — "
PLANO, ANGELO.	Cuba.	" — "
READ, WILLIAM G.	Baltimore.	" — "
RIGGS, GEORGE.	"	" — "
ROBINSON, GEORGE M.	Boston.	" — "
SERVARY, GABRIEL.	Baltimore.	" — "
SEWELL, RICHARD.	"	" — "
SPENCE, DECATUR.	"	" — "
WHITELY, LAMBERT A., A. M.	"	" —1842
BOURY, LEWIS J.	"	" —1839
BOURY, EDWARD A.	"	" — "
CAGE, DUNCAN S.	Mississippi.	" — "
CLEMENT, JAMES H.	Philadelphia.	" — "
CRAWFORD, JAMES.	Baltimore.	" — "
DE COURCY, WILLIAM.	Maryland.	" — "
DUNAN, LEWIS.	Baltimore.	" — "
FISHER, WILLIAM.	Philadelphia.	" — "
FRUSH, ALEXANDER.	Baltimore.	" — "
HEARD, DANIEL.	Texas.	" — "
HOLLINS, DUGAN.	Baltimore.	" —1840
HOWARD, GEORGE.	"	" — "
JENKINS, JOHN.	"	" —1839
LUSBY, ROBERT.	"	" — "
MCLANE, ALLAN.	Delaware.	" — "
OSWALD, THOMAS M.	Mississippi.	" — "
POWER, JOHN.	Baltimore.	" — "
SHAW, WILLIAM.	"	" — "
TILLINGHAST, WILLIAM.	Philadelphia.	" — "

NAME.	RESIDENCE.	ENTRY AND DEPARTURE.
WILSON, THOMAS.	Mobile.	1838—1839
ALSTON, MOTTE.	South Carolina.	" — "
BOUDOUSQUIE, LOUIS.	New Orleans.	" — "
BUCK, CHARLES.	Baltimore.	" — "
CHARTRAND, JOHN.	Matanzas.	" — "
GLOVER, JAMES.	New York.	" — "
GRISWOLD, DAVID.	Florida.	" — "
GRISWOLD, CHARLES.	"	" — "
HAYS, HENRY T., A. M.	Mississippi.	" —1841
HENRY, WILLIAM.	Philadelphia.	" —1839
HENRY, MORTON.	"	" — "
HOWARD, CHARLES R.	Baltimore.	" —1841
JOHNSTON, CHRISTOPHER.	"	" —1839
NABB, HENRY.	"	" — "
SIQUEIRA, ANTONIO DE.	Rio Janeiro.	" — "
TILGHMAN, STEDMAN.	Maryland.	" — "
WILKINS, JAMES.	Baltimore.	" — "
WRIGHT, RIGNALD.	"	" — "
DIAMOND, JOHN, A. B.	Philadelphia.	" —1840
GARESCHÉ, PETER BAUDUY, A. M.	Delaware.	" — "
HOUSTON, SAMUEL.	Baltimore.	" —1839
HOWARD, HAMILTON.	"	" — "
McCUTCHON, SAMUEL.	New Orleans.	" — "
McCUTCHON, PERCIVAL.	" "	" — "
ROBINSON, EDWARD W.	Philadelphia.	" —1840
SANCHEZ, JOSEPH C.	Malaga.	" —1839
WHELAN, GEORGE J.	Baltimore.	" — "
SHRIVER, JOHN ALEXANDER, A.M.	"	1839— "
BARKER, JOHN.	"	" —1840
BIRCKHEAD, HUGH.	"	" — "
BOEHM, JOHN L.	"	" — "
BOYLE, FRANCIS.	"	" — "
BOYLE, JAMES.	"	" — "
CADUC, PHILIP.	"	" —1841
CANONGE, EDGAR.	New Orleans.	" —1840
CARROLL, SAMUEL.	Baltimore.	" —1841
COCKEY, JOHN C.	"	" —1840

NAME.	RESIDENCE.	ENTRY AND DEPARTURE.
COCHRAN, OSCAR S.	Cuba.	1839—1840
DESELDING, FITZGERALD.	Baltimore.	" — "
DILLON, ASAHEL.	"	" — "
FETTERMAN, GEORGE, A. M.	Pittsburg.	" — "
HARDESTY, JAMES.	Baltimore.	" — "
HUGHLET, THOMAS.	Maryland.	" —1842
HOWARD, WILLIAM K.	Baltimore.	" —1840
HOWARD, WILLIAM R.	"	" —1841
JENKINS, MICHAEL.	"	" —1843
KELLY, FRANCIS.	"	" —1841
KING, SAMUEL.	"	" —1840
KRAFT, CHARLES.	"	" — "
LENDRUM, JOHN H.	"	" — "
MARROW, ISAAC.	"	" — "
MARSH, SAMUEL.	Philadelphia.	" — "
MCFAUL, M.	Baltimore.	" — "
MCFAUL, CHARLES.	"	" — "
MCLANE, CHARLES.	Delaware.	" — "
MENZIES, FRANCIS.	Baltimore.	" — "
MICHARD, HENRY.	"	" — "
MYERS, CHARLES.	"	" — "
NEALE, FRANCIS.	"	" —1841
O'DONNELL, JOHN.	"	" — "
POCHON, CHARLES.	"	" —1840
RINGGOLD, WILLIAM.	"	" —1841
ROBINSON, MATTHEW.	"	" —1840
SLINGLUFF, WILLIAM.	"	" — "
SLINGLUFF, RUBAN.	"	" — "
SPEAR, JOSEPH.	"	" — "
SPROSTON, JOHN.	"	" — "
STEWART, JAMES.	"	" —1841
SUTTON, THOMAS.	"	" —1840
WALTON, HENRY.	Philadelphia.	" — "
WAGGAMAN, EUGENE, A. B.	New Orleans.	" —1846
BARRY, ROBERT.	Baltimore.	" —1841
BARRY, SAMUEL.	"	" —1840
BOUVIER, EUSTACHE.	Philadelphia.	" — "

NAME.	RESIDENCE.	ENTRY AND DEPARTURE.
CHOTARD, HENRY.	Mississippi.	1839—1841
CHOTARD, RICHARD.	"	" — "
CORRIGAN, JOHN.	Baltimore.	" —1840
FETTERMAN, GILBERT.	Pittsburg.	" —1844
FRICK, FRANCIS, A. B.	Baltimore.	" —1845
HAYDEN, JAMES L.	"	" —1840
HOOK, HENRY.	"	" — "
HUGO, GEORGE T.	"	" — "
JENKINS, BRADFORD.	"	" —1842
LUCAS, GEORGE.	"	" —1841
MALLOY, JAMES.	"	" —1842
O"TOOLE, JOHN.	"	" —1840
PRICHARD, RICHARD.	New Orleans.	" —1842
SCOTT, MORRIS.	Baltimore.	" —1840
THOMPSON, ROBERT.	"	" — "
WOODVILLE, WILLIAM.	"	" —1841
BIRCKHEAD, JAMES.	"	" —1840
BLACKWOOD, WILLIAM.	"	" — "
BOURY, LEWIS.	"	" — "
FRICK, GEORGE, A. B.	"	" —1843
HARDESTY, JOHN.	"	" —1840
HART, FRANCIS.	"	" — "
HORWITZ, PHINEAS.	"	" — "
JACOBS, EMILE.	New Orleans.	" —1841
JOHNSON, REVERDY, A. B.	Baltimore.	" —1842
LAWN, JOHN.	"	" — "
LEVERING, CHARLES.	"	" —1840
McWILLIAMS, PATRICK.	"	" — "
MOALE, SAMUEL H.	"	" — "
MORGAN, GEORGE.	New York.	" — "
OSWALD, THOMAS.	Mississippi.	" — "
RAU, JOHN.	Baltimore.	" — "
ROBINSON, HENRY A.	"	" — "
ROBINSON, EDWARD G.	Boston.	" — "
SMITH, JOHN.	Baltimore.	" — "
SMITH, MARSHAL.	"	" — "
STOCKTON, RICHARD.	"	" — "

STUDENTS OF ST. MARY'S COLLEGE. 133

NAME.	RESIDENCE.	ENTRY AND DEPARTURE.
WEST, ARTHUR.	Maryland.	1839—1841
BERRYMAN, UPTON.	Baltimore.	" —1842
GETTINGS, HENRY.	"	" —1840
JAMES, WILLIAM.	Ohio.	" — "
MCKENZIE, THOMAS.	Baltimore.	" — "
O'DONNELL, LEWIS.	"	" — "
RAYMOND, S. SAMUEL.	Connecticut.	" — "
SHEPHERD, JOHN.	Charleston.	" — "
WHELAN, THOMAS, A. M.	Baltimore.	" —1842
ALDRIDGE, ANDREW.	"	" —1840
FISHER, WILLIAM W.	Philadelphia.	" — "
GLOVER, JAMES, A. M.	New York.	" — "
GRAFFLIN, CHRISTOPHER.	Baltimore.	" — "
HEPBURN, SAMUEL.	Washington.	" — "
MAUREAU, LOUIS O.	New Orleans.	" — "
SEMMES, IGNATIUS.	Maryland.	" — "
WICKERSHAM, WILLIAM.	Baltimore.	" — "
CAMPBELL, THOMAS.	"	1840—1841
CAMPBELL, GEORGE.	"	" —1845
CARRAVALLO, GABRIEL.	Matanzas.	" —1841
DUNLEVY, ANDREW.	Baltimore.	" — "
DELBERT, SIMON.	Bordeaux.	" — "
FOLEY, MATTHEW.	Baltimore.	" —1844
HILL, CLEMENT.	Maryland.	" —1841
HALL, FRANCIS.	"	" — "
HYDE, THEOPHILUS.	New Orleans.	" — "
INLOES, FRANCIS.	Baltimore.	" — "
JENKINS, IGNATIUS.	"	" —1842
KEENAN, JOSEPH.	"	" — "
MILLS, THOMAS.	"	" — "
MILLS, SYLVANUS.	"	" —1841
MUNCKS, HECTOR.	"	" — "
MARMILLION, NUMA.	New Orleans.	" — "
MERRITT, FRANCIS.	Baltimore.	" — "
PREVOST, FRANCIS.	"	" —1842
POCHON, CHARLES.	"	" —1846
POPHAM, JAMES.	New Orleans.	" —1841

NAME.	RESIDENCE.	ENTRY AND DEPARTURE.
Rodewald, John.	Baltimore.	1840—1841
Rodewald, Henry.	"	" — "
Scott, Morris.	"	" — "
Thorpe, William.	Martinique.	" — "
Walter, Jacob A.	Baltimore.	" — "
Williams, Francis.	"	" — "
Woodville, Middleton L.	"	" — "
Wysham, Henry C., A. B.	"	" —1847
Waterman, Thaddeus.	"	" —1841
Bryson, Francis, A. M.	"	" — "
Bean, John.	"	" — "
Bowie, Oden, A. M.	Maryland.	" —1845
Bouvier, Eustache.	Philadelphia.	" —1841
Cherbonnier, Victor.	Baltimore.	" — "
Cage, Albert.	Mississippi.	" — "
Gaskins, William.	Baltimore.	" — "
Hugo, G. S.	"	" — "
Hewitt, Cornelius P. T.	Philadelphia.	" — "
Hoffman, William.	Baltimore.	" — "
Mills, John.	"	" — "
Mills, William.	"	" — "
Marmillion, Ed. B.	New Orleans.	" — "
Madriz, Carlos.	Caraccas.	" — "
Perez, Ramon.	"	" — "
Pannell, Hugh.	Norfolk.	" — "
Riggs, George.	Baltimore.	" — "
Winder, James.	Maryland.	" — "
Barr, John C.	Baltimore.	" — "
Carey, Thomas.	"	" —1842
Fabre, Joseph.	Cuba.	" — "
Gosnel, Matthew.	Baltimore.	" —1841
Hodges, Wilson.	"	" — "
Jenkins, Felix, A. M.	"	" —1844
Patterson, Edward, A. B.	"	" — "
Thebaud, Edward.	New York.	" —1841
Yturbide, Augustine De.	Mexico.	" —1842
Arnoult, Theodule.	New Orleans.	" —1841

NAME.	RESIDENCE.	ENTRY AND DEPARTURE.
BUCKLER, JAMES.	Baltimore.	1840—1841
BEAN, JAMES C.	"	" — "
BENZINGER, FREDERIC.	"	" —1842
CLAYTON, JAMES.	Delaware.	" —1841
CAGE, DUNCAN.	Mississippi.	" — "
CORBIN, SIMS FRANCIS.	Philadelphia.	" — "
DARDENNE, JOHN A., A. M.	New Orleans.	" —1843
DESOBRY, HENRY, A. M.	"	" — "
HART, FRANCIS.	Baltimore.	" —1841
HINTON, WILLIAM.	North Carolina.	" — "
HINTON, EUGENE.	"	" — "
HEARD, DANIEL.	Natchitoches.	" — "
HITZELBERGER, CHARLES.	Baltimore.	" — "
HOSKINS, WILLIAM.	North Carolina.	" — "
LLOYD, HENRY.	" "	" — "
MAUND, REPOLD.	Baltimore.	" — "
OGSTON, GEORGE.	"	" — "
RODRIGUEZ, BERNABE.	Teneriffe.	" —1842
SLOAN, JAMES.	Baltimore.	" —1841
SHAW, WILLIAM C.	"	" — "
THOMPSON, ROBERT.	"	" — "
TAPPAN, ELI.	Ohio.	" —1842
WOODVILLE, R. CATON.	Baltimore.	" —1841
YTURBIDE, PHILLIP DE.	Mexico.	" — "
BAKER, ALFRED, A. B.	Baltimore.	" — "
BAKER, RICHARD.	North Carolina.	" — "
DAVIS, HUGH, A. B.	" "	" —1842
GLENN, WILLIAM, A. B.	Baltimore.	" —1841
LUSBY, CHARLES W., A. M.	"	" — "
JOHNSON, C.	"	" —1840
TRACEY, JAMES C., A. M.	"	" — "
BAUDUY, A. B.	Delaware.	" — "
BENNET, JAMES, A. B.	Baltimore.	1841—1847
BIZOUARD, ACHILLE.	"	" —1842
BLANCHE, THOMAS.	"	" — "
BAUGHER, ALEXIS J.	"	" — "
CARROLL, CHARLES.	"	" —1844

NAME.	RESIDENCE.	ENTRY AND DEPARTURE.
Clifton, Junius.	Baltimore.	1841—1842
Downs, Edward.	Mississippi.	" — "
Erney, Jacob.	Baltimore.	" — "
Figaniére, Frederic De.	New York.	" — "
Figaniére, William De.	"	" — "
Hickley, James.	Baltimore.	" — "
Harvey, Joshua.	"	" — "
Hooper, John.	"	" — "
Jamart, Louis.	"	" — "
Keenan, William.	"	" — "
Maund, Frederic.	"	" — "
Maund, George.	"	" — "
Myers, Charles.	"	" — "
Myers, Joseph.	"	" — "
McDonald, Hugh.	"	" — "
Rogers, William.	"	" — "
Taylor, Charles.	"	" — "
Tompkins, Joseph.	"	" — "
Torrance, Charles.	"	" — "
Vernon, William.	"	" — "
Wysham, Edward W.	"	" —1845
Crey, Frederic.	"	" —1842
Dillon, Asahel.	Ohio.	" —1844
Farrias, Casimiro.	Mexico.	" —1842
Farrias, Benito.	"	" — "
Goodwin, Edward, A. M.	Baltimore.	" —1846
Henry, William.	"	" —1842
Marsh, Samuel.	Philadelphia.	" — "
Rogers, Nathan.	Baltimore.	" — "
Sullivan, John.	"	" — "
Shenton, John.	Maryland.	" — "
Tubman, Richard.	"	" — "
Waters, Henry.	New Orleans.	" — "
Bowie, Oden, A. M.	Maryland.	" —1845
Cave, Charles.	Baltimore.	" —1842
Cherbonnier, Victor.	"	" — "
Dunlevy, Andrew.	"	" — "

NAME.	RESIDENCE.	ENTRY AND DEPARTURE.
EMORY, THOMAS.	Baltimore.	1841—1843
FRICK, FRANCIS.	"	" —1845
FERGUSON, JAMES.	"	" —1842
GREGG, ANDREW.	"	" — "
HAHN, DANIEL.	"	" — "
INGRAHAM, DUNCAN.	Philadelphia.	" — "
MADRIZ, CARLOS.	Caraccas.	" — "
McFAUL, MICHAEL.	Baltimore.	" — "
OGDEN, AMBROSE.	"	" — "
ROBINSON, MATHEW.	"	" — "
SUTTON, ROBERT, A. M.	"	" —1845
SCOTT, DANIEL.	Maryland.	" —1842
SMITH, ANTHONY.	Baltimore.	" — "
DANELS, JOSEPH.	"	" —1843
GLENN, JOHN.	"	" —1842
HICKLEY, ROBERT.	"	" — "
MARMILLION, EDMOND B.	New Orleans.	" —1843
MERCERET, LOUIS.	France.	" —1842
MERCERET, FRANCIS.	"	" — "
OGSTON, GEORGE.	Baltimore.	" —1844
OWINGS, JOHN.	"	" —1842
REED, BERNARD.	"	" — "
ROBINSON, GEORGE, A. M.	Boston.	" —1844
ROGERS, DANIEL.	Delaware.	" —1842
SMITH, MARSHALL J.	Virginia.	" — "
WHITE, ANDREW.	North Carolina.	" —1843
CLAYTON, CHARLES.	Delaware.	" —1842
FRISBY, JOHN.	Baltimore.	" — "
HODGES, WILSON.	"	" — ?
HEARD, DANIEL, A. B.	Natchitoches.	" —1842
HALL, WILLIAM.	Mississippi.	" — "
McKENZIE, THOMAS.	Baltimore.	" — "
MERRICK, RICHARD.	Maryland.	" — "
OSWALD, THOMAS.	Mississippi.	" — "
READ, JOHN D.	Delaware.	" — "
THOMAS, JOHN.	Maryland.	" — "
THOMAS, JAMES.	"	" — "

NAME.	RESIDENCE.	ENTRY AND DEPARTURE.
Miles, Oscar.	Maryland.	1841—1842
Shaw, William C.	Baltimore.	" — "
Sloan, James.	"	" — "
Brent, Charles.	Washington.	1842—1843
Bache, R. Meade.	Philadelphia.	" — "
Bujac, James.	Baltimore.	" — "
Birckhead, Hugh.	"	" — "
Balenzuela, José.	Havana.	" — "
Clifton, Junius.	Baltimore.	" — "
Dansac, Benjamin.	New Orleans.	" —1844
Depelet, Leon.	Martinique.	" — "
Gloninger, John.	Baltimore.	" — "
Griffin, Thomas.	"	" —1843
Godman, Henry.	Philadelphia.	" — "
Harwood, Henry.	Baltimore.	" — "
Hays, David.	"	" —1844
Hunter, Solomon H.	"	" —1845
Hill, Clement.	Maryland.	" —1844
Kemp, Charles.	Baltimore.	" — "
Kemp, Thomas.	"	" —1844
King, George.	"	" —1843
McAvoy, William.	"	" — "
Mullan, Edward.	"	" —1844
Neal, John.	"	" —1848
Renshaw, Frederic.	Caraccas.	" —1846
Rodewald, John.	Baltimore.	" —1843
Rogers, William.	"	" — ?
Schroeder, Charles, A. B.	"	" —1848
Smith, William.	Maryland.	" —1843
Tucker, St. George.	Delaware.	" — "
Vernon, William.	Baltimore.	" — "
Wilson, Edward.	"	" — "
Caduc, Philip.	"	" — "
Fetterman, George.	Pittsburg.	" — "
Gillingham, Charles.	Baltimore.	" — "
Hall, Francis.	Maryland.	" —1844
Hooper, John.	Baltimore.	" —1843

STUDENTS OF ST. MARY'S COLLEGE.

NAME.	RESIDENCE.	ENTRY AND DEPARTURE.
HENRY, WILLIAM.	Baltimore.	1842—1842
HYDE, THEOPHILUS.	New Orleans.	" — "
JOHNSON, WILLIAM.	Baltimore.	" —1843
KEMP, M.	"	" —1842
KNOT, LEON, A. M.	"	" —1847
LENNIG, FRANCIS.	Philadelphia.	" —1842
MARMILLION, NUMA.	New Orleans.	" —1846
MILLS, SYLVANUS.	Baltimore.	" —1843
MCHENRY, JAMES S.	"	" — "
O'DONNELL, EDMUND.	"	" — "
RATLIFF, DAVID.	Louisiana.	" —1842
RAYMO, FRANCIS W.	Baltimore.	" — "
STEWART, JAMES.	"	" —1844
SULLIVAN, JOHN.	"	" —1842
TUBMAN, RICHARD.	Maryland.	" — "
WALTER, JACOB A.	Baltimore.	" —1843
BOYLE, FRANCIS E., A. M.	"	" —1846
BOYLE, JAMES.	"	" —1843
COYLE, THOMAS W.	"	" — "
DURE, LEON.	Savannah.	" — "
HALL, KENT.	Baltimore.	" — "
INGRAHAM, DUNCAN.	Philadelphia.	" — "
JEWETT, JOSEPH.	Baltimore.	" — "
KING, SAMUEL.	"	" — "
LEE, JOHN.	Maryland.	" — "
MYERS, CHARLES.	Baltimore.	" — "
MCLOSKEY, JAMES.	Mobile.	" — "
NEALE, RAPHAEL F., A. B.	Maryland.	" —1846
NEALE, FRANCIS C., A. B.	Baltimore.	" — "
ROBERTSON, Z.	New Orleans.	" —1843
SMITH, ANTHONY M.	Baltimore.	" — "
TOOL, JOHN.	"	" — "
COAD, JOSEPH E., A. M.	Maryland.	" —1846
CREY, FREDERIC.	Baltimore.	" —1843
DESOBRY, LOUIS, A. B.	Louisiana.	" —1846
DOWNS, EDWARD.	Mississippi.	" —1844
DUPUY, OSCAR, A. B.	Louisiana.	" —1846

NAME.	RESIDENCE.	ENTRY AND DEPARTURE.
FABRÉ, JOSÉ.	San Jago de Cuba.	1842—1843
GAMIZ, GENERO.	Mexico.	" — "
GUIDRY, V.	Louisiana.	" — "
HART, FRANCIS.	Baltimore.	" —1844
HICKLEY, ROBERT.	"	" — "
HYLAND, WILLIAM L.	Maryland.	" — "
KELLY, FRANCIS, A. M.	Baltimore.	" —1846
MADDOX, JOSEPH H., A. M.	Maryland.	" —1843
MADDOX, GEORGE F.	"	" —1846
MARYE, S. B.	Virginia.	" —1845
NAVARETTE, MANUEL.	Mexico.	" —1843
PATTERSON, SAMUEL S., A. B.	Baltimore.	" —1846
PETIT, AMÉDEÉ, A. M.	Louisiana.	" — "
POSEY, FRANCIS M.	Maryland.	" —1843
REED, BERNARD, A. M.	Baltimore.	" —1846
SHENTON, JOHN R.	Maryland.	" —1844
SMITH, MARSHALL J.	Virginia.	1844—1843
TUCKER, CHARLES C.	Delaware.	1842—1844
WILSON, ROBERT, A. M.	Baltimore.	" —1846
BENZINGER, JOHN.	"	" —1843
BENNETT, MATTHEW.	"	" —1845
LEGARÉ, JAMES.	Charleston.	" —1844
BUCKLER, JAMES, A. B.	Baltimore.	" — "
LUCAS, GEORGE.	"	" — "
BAER, WARREN.	New Orleans.	1842
MILES, OSCAR, A. M.	Maryland.	"
RIORDAN, TIMOTHY, A. M.	Ireland.	"
SUMNER, JOHN S.	Baltimore.	"
ANDREWS, GEORGE.	Alabama.	1843—1844
BIZOUARD, ACHILLE.	Baltimore.	" —1846
CARROLL, JOHN.	Howard District.	" —1844
COE, WILLIAM G., A. M.	Baltimore.	" —1849
COX, JOSEPH.	"	" —1844
COX, WILLIAM.	"	" — "
DUHAMEL, WILLIAM.	"	" —1847
FLOYD, ROBERT.	"	" —1844
HART, WILLIAM.	Louisiana.	" — "

NAME.	RESIDENCE.	ENTRY AND DEPARTURE.
HORWITZ, BENJAMIN.	Baltimore.	1843—1844
HOFFMAN, HENRY.	"	" — "
MEDCALF, ADDISON.	"	" — "
McKEW, EDWARD.	"	" — "
McMULLEN, JOHN.	"	" — "
MILLS, ROBERT.	"	" — "
O'DONOVAN, CHARLES, A. B.	"	" —1850
SCHWARTZ, JOHN.	"	" —1844
TIFFANY, GEORGE.	"	" — "
TOLEDANO, ERNEST.	New Orleans.	" — "
WYSHAM, KEMP.	Baltimore.	" — "
JAMART, LOUIS.	Baltimore.	1843—1844
JENKINS, IGNATIUS.	"	" — "
HICKLEY, JAMES.	"	" —1846
McKEW, DENNIS, A. M.	"	" —1848
McDONALD, HUGH.	"	" —1845
LENNIG, FRANCIS.	Philadelphia.	" —1844
RAYMO, FRANCIS W.	Baltimore.	" — "
SOBRINO, MATEO.	Yucatan.	" — "
TORRENCE, CHARLES.	Baltimore.	" — "
BOURNE, THOMAS B.	Maryland.	" — "
DENMEAD, TALBOTT.	Baltimore.	" — "
ELLICOTT, EVANS.	"	" — "
GUEL, FRANCIS.	Havana.	" — "
HERRERA, RAMON.	Guayaquil.	" — "
KEENAN, JOSEPH.	Baltimore.	" — "
McLANE, CHARLES.	Delaware.	" — "
MEDCALF, ADDISON.	Baltimore.	" — "
McFAUL, CHARLES.	"	" — "
McLOSKEY, JOHN.	Alabama.	" — "
ROSSIGNOL, HENRY.	Georgia.	" — "
SMITH, WILLIAM.	Maryland.	" — "
ANDREWS, JOHN J.	Alabama.	" — "
BOLAND, MICHAEL.	Georgia.	" — "
DUNNECK, JOHN.	Maryland.	" — "
DUPUY, GIDEON.	Louisiana.	" — "
EDWARD, JAMES.	Baltimore.	" — "

NAME.	RESIDENCE.	ENTRY AND DEPARTURE.
Getty, William.	Baltimore.	1843—1844
Harwood, David.	"	" — "
Holmes, George.	"	" — "
Lanahan, Thomas, A. M.	"	" —1846
McHenry, James.	"	" —1844
Menier, John.	Louisiana.	" — "
Posey, Francis M.	Maryland.	" — "
Rich, Arthur, A. M.	Baltimore.	" —1846
Robinson, Matthew, A. M.	"	" — "
Tubman, Richard.	Maryland.	" —1844
Baker, Maurice.	Baltimore.	" — "
Coad, Joseph E.	Maryland.	" —1845
Kenny, John.	Virginia.	" —1844
Thomas, William.	Maryland.	" — "
Maddox, Joseph H., A. B.	"	" — "
Calder, Alexander.	Scotland.	? —1843
Glover, Robert, A. M.	New York.	? — "
Pritchard, Richard.	Louisiana.	? — "
Leaumont, R. De, A. M.	Charleston.	? — "
Barry, William R.	Baltimore.	1844—1845
Brown, James.	"	" — "
Broadbent, John Scotti.	"	" — "
Butler, John.	"	" —1846
Child, Samuel.	"	" — "
Cloutier, Jean Baptiste.	Louisiana.	" —1848
Cloutier, Edward.	"	" — "
Cromwell, Richard.	Baltimore.	" —1845
Cox, Joseph.	"	" — "
Cox, William.	"	" —1851
Crummer, Daniel.	"	" — "
Foley, John, A. B.	"	" — "
Freeland, John H.	"	" —1845
Heuisler, Joseph.	"	" — "
Hoffman, Henry.	"	" — "
Howard, James.	"	" — "
Kelly, William H.	"	" —1848
Laroque, Francis.	"	" —1845

RT. REV. AUGUSTIN VEROT, D. D.,
First Bishop of St. Augustine, Fla.

NAME.	RESIDENCE.	ENTRY AND DEPARTURE.
McFaul, Francis.	Baltimore.	1844—1845
Marmillion, Valsin.	Louisiana.	" —1847
McKew, Edward.	Baltimore.	" —1845
O'Donovan, John H.	"	" —1847
Peterson, Joseph.	"	" —1850
Prudhomme, Gabriel.	Louisiana.	" —1848
Prudhomme, Emile.	"	" — "
Slater, William J., A. B.	Baltimore.	" —1851
Stewart, John.	"	" —1846
Tiffany, George.	"	" — ?
Toledano, Ernest.	Louisiana.	" —1845
Tucker, St. George.	Delaware.	" — "
West, Benjamin F.	Baltimore.	" — "
Antunez, Joachim.	Alabama.	" —1846
Bayard, B. Richard.	Delaware.	" —1845
Howard, John.	Baltimore.	" — "
Howard, Charles.	"	" — "
Jamart, Louis.	"	" — "
Kemp, William J.	"	" — "
Knox, Joseph J.	Alabama.	" —1846
Muncks, Edward.	Baltimore.	" — "
Prudhomme, P. J. Lestan.	Louisiana.	" —1848
Saunders, Phineas B.	Baltimore.	" —1845
Torrence, Charles.	"	" — "
Wysham, Kemp.	"	" — "
Brown, Amos P.	Maryland.	" — "
Christ, Jacob.	Pennsylvania.	" — "
De Figaniere, William.	Philadelphia.	" — "
Griffith, Nicholas R.	Maryland.	" — "
Jenkins, John, A. B.	Baltimore.	" —1849
Lennig, Francis.	Philadelphia.	" —1845
McCloskey, John.	Alabama.	" — "
McLane, Charles.	Delaware.	" — "
Riccards, John.	"	" — "
Coyle, Thomas W.	Baltimore.	" —1847
Easter, William.	Baltimore.	" —1845
Emory, Augustine.	Baltimore.	" — "

NAME.	RESIDENCE.	ENTRY AND DEPARTURE.
Gallaway, John.	Maryland.	1844—1845
Fernandez, Ramon.	Havana.	" — "
Fernandez, Pedro.	Havana.	" — "
Lindsay, Beverly.	Philadelphia.	" — "
Marmillion, Edmund B.	Louisiana.	" —1846
Miligan, Bayard.	Louisiana.	" —1845
Roach, Benjamin.	Mississippi.	" —1847
Travers, William H., A. M.	Virginia.	" —1851
Walter, Jacob A., A. B.	Baltimore.	" — "
Vickers, George J.	Maryland.	" —1847
Downy, William.	Baltimore.	" —1845
Gareshé, John.	Delaware.	" — "
Jones, William.	Mississippi.	" — "
Howard, Francis.	Baltimore.	" — "
Lacroix, Charles.	Montreal.	" — "
Rossignol, Henry.	Georgia.	" — "
Segur, Emile.	Louisiana.	" — "
Read, James.	Baltimore.	1844—1845
Waters, Francis, A. M.	Baltimore.	" — "
Dunneck, John.	Maryland.	1844
Hickley, Robert.	Baltimore.	"
King, Francis, A. M.	Pennsylvania.	"
Marmillion, Edmund.	Louisiana.	"
Taché, Vinceslas.	Quebec.	"
Waters, John, A. B.	Baltimore.	"
Bull, Thomas W.	New York.	1845—1848
Butler, William.	Baltimore.	" —1846
D'Ouville, Edward H.	Guadaloupe.	" — "
Dennis, James.	Maryland.	" — ?
Doize, Armand.	Baltimore.	" —1850
Drohan, David.	"	" —1848
Fisher, Lewis.	"	" —1851
Gallagher, Francis P. J.	"	" —1848
Henderson, John.	"	" —1846
King, Thomas.	"	" — "
Jenkins, Thomas Courtney.	"	" — "
Lebrun, Alphonse.	Guadaloupe.	" — "

STUDENTS OF ST. MARY'S COLLEGE.

NAME.	RESIDENCE.	ENTRY AND DEPARTURE.
LEBRUN, CONSTANT.	Guadaloupe.	1845—1846
NETH, LEWIS.	Baltimore.	" — "
PITMAN, EDWARD.	"	" — "
POCHON, JULES.	"	" —1851
QUIMLAN, CHARLES H.	"	" —1846
QUIMLAN, JAMES.	"	" — "
STEWART, DONALDSON.	"	" — "
TRACY, JOHN.	"	" — "
TAYLOR, DANIEL.	"	" —1847
WELSH, THOMAS.	"	" — "
CLIFTON, LEWIS.	"	" — "
DELAIGLE, LOUIS.	Georgia.	" — "
FLOYD, ROBERT.	Baltimore.	" — "
GOLDSMITH, ROBERT, A. B.	"	" —1851
GOULD, WILLIAM H.	"	" —1847
McMULLAN, JOHN.	"	" — "
RENSHAW, LOUIS.	Caraccas.	" —1848
RENSHAW, ROBERT.	"	" — "
TAYLOR, GEORGE.	Baltimore.	" —1847
COLLINS, CHARLES.	Alabama.	" —1846
DESDIER, FREDERICK.	Havana.	" —1847
DUHURST, JOHN.	Baltimore.	" —1846
JENKINS, JOHN.	"	" —1848
KING, GEORGE.	"	" —1846
MULLAN, EDWARD.	"	" — "
STINCHCOMB, JOHN.	"	" —1847
TORRENCE, CHARLES.	"	" —1846
VALETTE, JEROME CONSTANTINE.	"	" — "
VANCE, STANLEY.	Louisiana.	" — "
WALTER, JAMES.	Baltimore.	" — "
WARNER, MICHAEL.	"	" — "
WARNER, GEORGE K.	"	" — "
DE BUTTS, JOHN.	"	" — "
DENMEAD, FRANCIS.	"	" — "
HORWITZ, BENJAMIN.	"	" — "
O'DONOVAN, CHARLES.	"	" — "
TRAVERS, HENRY.	"	" — "

SEMINARY OF ST. SULPICE.

NAME.	RESIDENCE.	ENTRY AND DEPARTURE.
Castellanos, Henry C., A. M.	Louisiana.	1845—1847
Eccleston, John, A. M.	Maryland.	" — "
De Las Heras, Bernardo.	Guayaquil.	" —1847
Stewart, James, A. M.	Baltimore.	" —1848
Willcox, Joseph.	Delaware.	" —1846
Galligher, Michael.	Frederick.	" —1847
Herrera, Ramon.	Guayaquil.	" —1846
Willcox, John.	Delaware.	" — "
Vance, Gilbert.	Louisiana.	" —1847
Denmead, Talbott.	Baltimore.	1845
Gaiennié, Dennis.	Louisiana.	"
McNerhany, Edward, A. B.	Washington.	"
McCloskey, James.	Alabama.	"
Bull, George.	New York.	1846—1848
Coyle, John.	Baltimore.	" — "
Curly, James.	"	" —1847
Carrere, William.	"	" —1848
Donelan, William.	Washington.	" — "
Fernandez, Geronimo.	Caraccas.	" — "
Gosnell, William.	Baltimore.	" —1847
Hinson, George.	"	" —1848
Haydel, George.	Louisiana.	" — "
Haydel, Belford.	"	" — "
Hale, Thomas.	New Orleans.	" — "
Hart, Henry J.	Baltimore.	" — "
Jenkins, Albert S.	"	" —1851
Keirle, Nathaniel G.	"	" —1847
King, Joseph.	"	" — "
McManus, Felix.	"	" — "
Parrott, William.	Washington.	" —1848
Perry, Felix.	Baltimore.	" —1847
Stewart, Donaldson.	"	" — "
Slack, J. H.	"	" — "
Walker, Patrick.	"	" —1848
Walker, Noah Dixon.	"	" — "
Boyle, Edward A.	"	" —1847
Boyle, John P.		" — "

NAME.	RESIDENCE.	ENTRY AND DEPARTURE.
ELLIS, CLINTON.	St. Louis.	1846—1847
LAROQUE, EDWARD.	Baltimore.	" — "
HART, MANLY.	"	" — "
HART, HENRY.	"	" — "
HEUISLER, STANISLAUS.	"	" — ?
JONES, WILLIAM.	Mississippi.	1846—1847
MYERS, JOHN.	Baltimore.	" — "
MULLIN, JAMES.	"	" —1848
O'DONNELL, COLUMBUS.	"	" —1847
RICH, THOMAS.	"	" — "
SECHE, JOSEPH.	"	" —1848
STEWART, JAMES.	"	" — "
BELL, JOHN.	"	" — "
DUCATEL, JULIUS.	"	" — ?
FLOYD, ROBERT.	Maryland.	" —1849
GOULD, WILLIAM.	Baltimore.	" —1847
GLONINGER, JOHN.	"	" — "
GREENWOOD, CHARLES.	Virginia.	" — "
GREEN, EDWARD J.	Baltimore.	" — "
GREEN, ROBERT F.	"	" — "
HEUISLER, JOSEPH.	"	" — "
HOOPER, JAMES.	"	" —1849
HOWE, CHARLES.	Boston.	" —1847
HUNTER, SOLOMON H.	Baltimore.	" —1848
MALLEN, THOMAS.	"	" —1847
SAUNDERS, PHINEAS B.	"	" —1848
SPARROW, LOUIS.	Maryland.	" —1849
TAYLOR, GEORGE.	Baltimore.	" — "
TORRENCE, CHARLES.	"	" —1847
WYSHAM, KEMP.	"	" — "
WEGNER, FREDERICK.	"	" —1848
FERNANDEZ, JOSE.	Caraccas.	" —1849
FERNANDEZ, LADISLAO.	"	" — "
FERNANDEZ, MELICIO.	"	" —1847
GOULD, WILLIAM H.	Baltimore.	" — "
RABORG, FREDERICK.	Peru.	" —1848
SETZE, EUGENE.	Georgia.	" —1849

NAME.	RESIDENCE.	ENTRY AND DEPARTURE.
VICKERS, JAMES.	Maryland.	1846—1847
BOWIE, WILLIAM D.	"	" — "
HOWE, CHARLES.	Boston.	" — "
ELLIS, WILLIAM H. C., A. B.	St. Louis.	" — "
GARESHÉ, FRANCIS, A. B.	Delaware.	" — "
ROUBIEU, PASCHALIS.	Louisiana.	" — "
BUAR, ALCIDE, A. B.	"	1846
CARICO, THOMAS.	Maryland.	"
HUBERT, STEPHEN.	"	"
RAGGIO, ANTONIO.	Italy.	"
BANKS, GEORGE W.	Baltimore.	1847—1848
BARRY, PHILIP.	"	" — "
BROOKE, FRANK.	"	" —1851
DOYLE, THOMAS J.	"	" —1848
SADTLER, C. COLUMBUS.	"	" — "
MCARDEL, JOHN.	"	" — "
MCKEEVER, JOHN.	"	" —1850
MONTGOMERY, THOMAS F.	Natchez.	" —1848
PEARSON, JAMES.	Baltimore.	" — "
PREVOT, FRANCIS.	"	" — "
ROSENTHAL, LOUIS.	"	" — "
SLATTER, HENRY.	"	" — "
WALKER, GEORGE.	"	" —1850
WELSH, FRANCIS.	"	" —1848
DELAIGLE, CARLOS.	Georgia.	" — "
FITZPATRICK, HENRY.	Baltimore.	" — "
FORSTALL, EMILE.	New Orleans.	" — "
GOODWIN, BRADFORT.	Maine.	" —1851
HALLERS, WILLIAM.	Baltimore.	" —1848
HELLEN, JAMES.	"	" — "
KENNEDY, G. R. S.	New Orleans.	" — "
KENNARD, THOMAS A.	Baltimore.	" — "
LAROQUE, FRANCIS.	"	" — "
MARTIN, ROBERT K., A. B.	"	" —1852
MCDONNELL, AMBROSE A.	"	" —1848
NEALE, STEPHEN.	Maryland.	". — "
POCHON, JULES.	Baltimore.	" —1851

NAME.	RESIDENCE.	ENTRY AND DEPARTURE.
SAUVÉ, HENRY, A. B.	New Orleans.	1847—1852
ALDRIDGE, JOHN.	Baltimore.	" —1848
CHASE, CHARLES M.	"	" — "
DA ROCHA, JOSE BATISTA.	Brazil.	" — "
DENNIS, JAMES.	Maryland.	" — "
DUCATEL, JULIUS.	Baltimore.	" — "
HAND, EDWARD, A. B.	"	" —1851
HEUISLER, JOSEPH.	"	" —1848
HOOPER, JAMES.	"	" — "
McKEW, EDWARD.	"	" — "
MILLS, ROBERT.	"	" — "
NORRIS, JOHN B.	"	" — "
SHANNESY, HENRY.	?	" — "
BORGES, DOMINGO.	Havana.	" — "
BROADFOOT, J. A.	Baltimore.	" — "
DELAIGLE, LOUIS.	Georgia.	" — "
COX, JOSEPH.	Baltimore.	" — "
CUNNINGHAM, CHARLES A. D.	"	" — "
FENWICK, EDWARD.	Maryland.	" — "
McKENNA, JOSEPH.	Ireland.	" — "
SALVADORES, ANGELO.	Porto Rico.	" — "
WINN, JOHN.	Baltimore.	" — "
BIENVENU, PLACIDE.	Louisiana.	" — "
CLARK, JOHN.	Maryland.	" — "
CORNAY, T. H.	Louisiana.	" — ?
DORSEY, RUBEN.	Maryland.	" —1848
HAMBLETON, THOMAS E., A. B.	Baltimore.	" —1849
LAMBREMONT, PIERRE.	Louisiana.	" —1848
LEARY, THOMAS.	North Carolina.	" — "
MITCHELL, JOHN G.	Maryland.	" — "
MURREL, JOHN C.	Mobile.	" — "
OLIVIER, OSCAR.	Louisiana.	" — "
VANCE, STANLEY.	New Orleans.	" — "
VILLERÉ, CHARLES, A. B.	" "	" —1849
WARNER, GEORGE K., A. B.	Baltimore.	" — "
WINN, JOHN.	"	" —1848
SUTTON, JOHN.	"	" — "

NAME.	RESIDENCE.	ENTRY AND DEPARTURE.
GALLIGHER, MICHAEL, A. M.	Maryland.	1847
MCMANUS, BERNARD.	Pennsylvania.	"
MCNALLY, JOHN.	Baltimore.	"
NORRIS, JOHN.	Washington.	"
RENSHAW, FREDERICK.	Caraccas.	"
O'BRIEN, EDWARD.	Baltimore.	"
ROGER, THOMAS L., A. M.	Charleston.	1847—1848
PREVOST, EURIALE.	Baltimore.	" — "
BAKER, JOSEPH.	"	1848—1852
BANKS, ANDREW.	"	" —1849
BANKS, CHARLES W.	"	" — "
BERRYMAN, JOHN.	"	" —1852
BETHELL, WILLIAM.	Louisiana.	" —1849
BEVAN, GEORGE F.	Maryland.	" — "
CHESTNUT, WASHINGTON.	Baltimore.	" — "
CHENASSÉ, JOHN.	"	" —1852
CONNOLLY, THOMAS.	"	" —1851
FRUSH, CHARLES W.	"	" —1849
HALL, THOMAS.	"	" — "
HENDLEY, WILLIAM H.	"	" — "
KERNAN, PETER.	"	" — "
LOVE, RICHARD J. W.	"	" — "
LOVE, WILLIAM.	"	" — "
MCPHERSON, MAYNARD.	"	" —1851
RECKER, WILLIAM.	"	" —1849
ROACH, THOMAS F.	"	" — "
ROSENSWIG, ABRAHAM, SR.	"	" — "
ROSENSWIG, ABRAHAM, JR.	"	" — "
THOMPSON, ALFRED.	"	" —1852
WRIGHT, DANIEL GÉRAUD.	"	" —1849
WAMBERNIE, JOHN EDWARD.	Charleston.	" — "
WILSON, FREDERICK.	Baltimore.	" — "
CARR, WILSON R.	Maryland.	" — "
CLARK, JOHN R.	Baltimore.	" — "
CONNOLLY, JOHN B.	"	" — "
HASSELBERGER, LOUIS.	"	" — "
HOPKINS, JOHN F.	"	" —1850

NAME.	RESIDENCE.	ENTRY AND DEPARTURE.
JONES, FRANCIS.	Baltimore.	1848—1851
MCELROY, JOHN.	"	" —1849
O'DONOVAN, EDWARD.	"	" — "
ROSENTHAL, LOUIS.	"	" — "
RICH, WILLIAM.	"	" — "
STEWARD, DAVID.	"	" — "
WRIGHT, GUSTAVUS W. F.	"	" — "
BOYD, THEODORE.	Cuba.	" — "
CARLIN, ALBERT.	Louisiana.	" — "
CURLEY, JAMES.	Baltimore.	" — "
DE MONTALVO, LINO.	Cuba.	" — "
HART, MANLY.	Baltimore.	" — "
KENNARD, THOMAS R.	"	" — "
LIVINGSTONE, DE GRASSE.	New York.	" — "
LIVINGSTONE, ROBERT.	"	" — "
ROBERTS, WILLIAM.	Baltimore.	" — "
RUDDICK, EDMUND.	"	" — "
STAPLETON, MAXIMILIAN.	"	" — "
WITMAN, WILLIAM F.	"	" —1851
ANTUNEZ, JOACHIM.	Mobile.	" —1849
BARTLETT, EDWARD.	Cuba.	" — "
BOYD, THEODORE.	"	" — "
CLOUD, WILLIAM P.	Baltimore.	" — "
CORNAY, FLORIAN.	Louisiana.	" — "
DICKEY, CHARLES E.	Baltimore.	" — "
DARBY, JOHN N.	Maryland.	" — "
DÉSOBRY, CHARLES.	Louisiana.	" — "
ESHBACH, JOSEPH.	Baltimore.	" —1852
JONES, AUBREY A., A. B.	"	" —1851
KEMP, CHARLES.	"	" —1849
KEMP, THOMAS.	"	" — "
LABAUVE, ODILON.	Louisiana.	" — "
LIVINGSTONE, WALTER.	New York.	" — "
MCMULLEN, JOHN F.	Baltimore.	" —1852
MUMMA, EDWARD.	"	" —1849
O'DONOVAN, CHARLES.	"	" —1852
POULSON, THOMAS H. J.	"	" —1849

NAME.	RESIDENCE.	ENTRY AND DEPARTURE.
RICH, THOMAS.	Baltimore.	1848—1849
WAGNER, HENRY C.	"	" — "
BERNADU, JOHN C.	Philadelphia.	" — "
BROUSSARD, PRÉVAL.	Louisiana.	" — "
DEJEAN, A.	"	" — "
HOMANS, THOMAS S.	Baltimore.	" — "
PHILLIPS, ALFRED.	Louisiana.	" — "
ESHBACH, JOHN.	Baltimore.	" — "
PATTERSON, ROBERT, A. B.	"	" — "
SUTTON, ANDREW J., A. M.	"	1848
WILLIAMS, SAMUEL F.	"	"
BELT, BENJAMIN.	Washington.	"
HENNIS, HENRY S.	Philadelphia.	"
O'GRADY, MICHAEL.	Ireland.	"
WATERS, JOHN.	Baltimore.	"
ARNOLD, SAMUEL.	?	1848—1849
BONN, H. L.	?	" — "
BROWN, OWEN.	?	" — "
MARTIN, J. M.	?	" — "
GREMM, JAMES.	?	" — "
GOLDSBOROUGH, RICHARD.	?	" — "
HIGGINS, EDWARD.	?	" — "
HANNITY, JOHN.	?	" — "
KREMS, JOSEPH.	?	" — "
SMITH, CONSTANT.	?	" — "
VAN CAMP, EUGENE.	?	" — "
LATROBE, OSMUN.	Baltimore.	? — ?
KERNAN, EUGENE.	?	1849—1850
TIERNAN, FRANCIS.	Baltimore.	" — "
TRAVERS, JOSEPH.	Virginia.	" — "
BAER, JAMES.	Baltimore.	1850—1851
BELL, GEORGE W.	"	" — "
BENNETT, THOMAS.	"	" — "
BETTON, JOEL W.	"	" — "
BRADY, JOHN W.	"	" — "
CABEZAS, FRANCIS G.	Havana.	" — "
CAFFERY, DONALSON.	Louisiana.	" — "

STUDENTS OF ST. MARY'S COLLEGE.

NAME.	RESIDENCE.	ENTRY AND DEPARTURE.
CASTELLANOS, JOHN J., A. B.	New Orleans.	1850—1852
CHASSAING, EDWARD.	Baltimore.	" — "
CHASSAING, HENRY.	"	" — "
CLARKE, GEORGE.	"	" —1851
CONNOLLY, WILLIAM.	Montreal.	" — "
CARBON, CHARLES.	Baltimore.	" — "
COOKE, FREDERICK.	"	" — "
CORNETTE, ARMAND.	"	" — "
CRANE, CHARLES.	"	" — "
CREY, FREDERICK.	"	" — "
CROMWELL, RICHARD.	"	" — "
DENISON, HENRY C.	"	" — "
DOIZE, LUCIEN.	"	" — "
ELDER, P. LAURENSON.	"	" — "
ESCOBAR, RICHARD.	Panama.	" — "
FISHER, RICHARD, A. B.	Baltimore.	" — "
FISHER, ROBERT, A. B.	"	" — "
FICKEY, ROBERT.	"	" — "
FITZGERALD, RICHARD.	"	" — "
FRENCH, E.	"	" — "
FRENCH, JULES.	"	" — "
FREY, JAMES L.	"	" — "
GAITHER, BRADLEY.	"	" — ?
GARVEY, WILLIAM.	"	" —1851
GOSNELL, WILLIAM.	"	" — "
GIMBERNAT, FLORENTINE.	Porto Rico.	" — "
GIMBERNAT, JOSEPH.	" "	" — "
GRAVES, ROSEWELL H., A. B.	Baltimore.	" — "
GRAVES, WILLIAM.	"	" — "
HAMBLETON, FRANCIS H.	"	" — "
HANDLY, W. H.	"	" — "
HOOVER, FRANCIS.	"	" — "
HOUGH, W. D.	"	" — "
HYDE, JAMES.	"	" — "
HULL, JOSEPH J.	"	" — "
INGERSOLL, CHARLES J.	"	1850
JAMISON, BENJAMIN.	"	1850—1851

NAME.	RESIDENCE.	ENTRY AND DEPARTURE.
JENKINS, THOMAS C., JR., A. B.	Baltimore.	1850—1851
JEFFREY, JOHN T.	St. Louis.	" — "
KELLY, CHARLES.	Baltimore.	" — "
KERNAN, EUGENE.	"	" — "
KREBS, H. B.	"	" — "
LAYAT, MICHAEL, A. B.	New York.	" —1852
LATROBE, CHARLES H.	Baltimore.	" —1851
MUCHADO, JOHN.	Caraccas.	" — "
MAYER, LEWIS.	Baltimore.	" — "
MILHOLLAND, E.	"	" — "
M'LAUGHLIN, A.	"	" — "
M'LAUGHLIN, WM.	"	" — "
MCMANUS, FELIX.	"	" — "
MCSHERRY, JAMES W.	Virginia.	" — "
MONTAGU, CHARLES.	Ireland.	" — "
NICHOLSON, CHARLES G.	Baltimore.	" — "
NICHOLSON, JOHN H. R.	"	" — "
NAVY, GEORGE W.	"	" — "
O'BRIEN, W. J.	"	" — "
OSIO, ANTONIO.	Mexico.	" — "
OSIO, SALVADOR.	"	" — "
PARKHURST, DANIEL.	Baltimore.	" — "
PLUNKETT, JAMES.	"	" — "
POE, JOHN P.	"	" — "
POE, NELSON.	"	" — "
REIP, JOSEPH H.	"	" — "
ROSENTHAL, LEWIS.	"	" — "
SADTLER, CHARLES.	"	" — "
SHANNESSY, JAMES.	"	" — "
SERVARY, F. CHATARD.		" — "
SOMERVILLE, ROBERT.	"	" — "
SOMERVILLE, JOSEPH.	"	" — "
SMITH, WILLIAM.	"	" — "
STEWART, JAMES H.	"	" — "
SPROSTON, GEORGE S.	"	" — "
SPROSTON, W. G.	"	" — "
WARNER, GEORGE, A. M.	"	" — "

STUDENTS OF ST. MARY'S COLLEGE. 155

NAME.	RESIDENCE.	ENTRY AND DEPARTURE.
WARNER, WILLIAM.	Baltimore.	1850—1851
WARD, W. MURRAY, A. M.	"	" — "
WEGNER, CHARLES.	"	" — "
WILLIAMS, OSCAR.	"	" — "
WHITE, JOHN CHARLES.	"	" — "
WHITE, THOMAS H.	"	" — "
WRIGHT, ROBERT N.	"	" — "
ZANE, S. SPRIGG.	Wheeling.	" — "
BAER, ARTHUR.	Baltimore.	" —1852
BALDWIN, E. F.	"	" — "
BAXLEY, CLAUDE.	"	" — "
BROWN, C. C.	Maryland.	" — "
CAFFRY, JOHN T.	Baltimore.	" — "
CARROLL, ALBERT.	Maryland.	" — "
CARROLL, R. G. HARPER.	"	" — "
CALDWELL, A. P.	Baltimore.	1851— ?
CALDWELL, W. Q.	"	" —1852
CHATARD, P. T.	"	" — "
CORBON, CHARLES.	"	" — "
CORNETTE, MELCHOIR.	"	" — "
COAD, W. R.	Maryland.	" — "
COLLINS, GEORGE T.	Pittsburg.	" — "
COFFIELD, EUGENE F.	Baltimore.	" — ?
CLOUD, JESSE L.	"	" — ?
CRAIG, JOHN C.	Pennsylvania.	" — ?
DENMEAD, E.	Baltimore.	" — ?
DENMEAD, B. F.	"	" — ?
DORSEY, LOUIS W.	"	" — ?
DUMONT, A.	"	" — ?
ESPIN, R.	Cuba.	" — ?
EDELIN, BENJAMIN M.	Maryland.	" — ?
FISCHER, LEWIS.	Baltimore.	" — ?
GARDENER, F. D.	Maryland.	" —1852
GARDENER, R. H.	"	" — "
GILL, ELI.	Baltimore.	" — "
GILL, SAMUEL H.	"	" — "
GLOVER, EDWARD A.	New York.	" — "

NAME.	RESIDENCE.	ENTRY AND DEPARTURE.
Hambleton, F. H.	Baltimore.	1851— ?
Heighe, W. J.	"	" — ?
Hoops, W. P.	"	" —1852
Jenkins, C. Kennedy.	"	" — "
Jenkins, Thomas W.	"	" — "
Jones, Joshua.	"	" — "
Juara, Thomas.	Havana.	" — "
La Roche, C. Percy.	Philadelphia.	" — "
Layat, Michael.	New York.	" — "
Lee, Richard Henry.	Baltimore.	" — "
Lee, C. Carroll.	"	" — ?
Lizé, Alexander.	"	" —1852
Lowry, H. P.	"	" — ?
Lurman, J. S.	"	" —1852
Lemmon, William.	"	" — "
Maffei, Angelo.	"	" — ?
Mason, Samuel.	"	" — ?
Marye, W. A.	"	" —1852
Mayer, Alfred M.	"	" — "
McGarey, P.	Virginia.	" — "
M'Glone, Bernard.	Baltimore.	" — "
Moore, P. Henry.	Virginia.	" — "
Myers, A. M.	Baltimore.	" — ?
Pittman, J. R.	"	" — ?
Schmidt, L. V.	"	" —1852
Sadtler, Charles.	"	" — ?
Smith, T. H.	"	" —1852
Steuart, R. S. F.	"	" — "
Steiger, B. F.	Washington, D. C.	" — "
Stinchcomb, J. N.	Baltimore.	" — "
Thomas, E. O.	"	" — "
Travers, W. H.	"	" — "
Webb, G. W.	"	" — "
West, W. C.	"	" — ?
Wolfe, N. S.	"	" — ?
Zane, Edmund P.	Virginia.	" —1852
Zane, Eugene C.	"	" — "

NAME.	RESIDENCE.	YEAR.
ANDERSON, IJETT. W.	Baltimore.	1852
ANDERSON, JOHN K.	"	"
ANDERSON, WILLIAM WEMGS.	"	"
BENITES, RAPHAEL.	Panama.	"
BROADBENT, FERDINAND.	Baltimore.	"
BROADBENT, STEPHEN.	"	"
BROGDEN, ARTHUR.	"	"
BUCHANAN, DAVID.	"	"
BUCHANAN, JAMES M.	"	"
CARROLL, JOSEPH.	"	"
CHATARD, F. P.	"	"
CLAUTICE, WILLIAM F.	"	"
COLLINS, JAMES E.	"	"
COONEY, WILLIAM J.	"	"
CREY, H. J.	"	"
DEVRIES, W. R.	"	"
DOBBIN, JOSEPH C.	"	"
DOIZE, L.	"	"
DOWNEY, LAWSON.	"	"
EICHELBERGER, F. C.	"	"
EICHELBERGER, JOHN C.	"	"
FISHER, H.	"	"
FISHER, WILLIAM.	"	"
FRANCIS, A. G.	Cincinnati.	"
GARDINER, F. D.	Maryland.	"
GIBBONS, FRANCIS.	Baltimore.	"
GOULON, ALPHONSE.	"	"
GRAFF, J. H.	"	"
GRAVES, H. M.	"	"
GRAVES, WILLIAM.	"	"
GRIFFITH, G. S.	"	"
GUERAND, EUGENE.	"	"
HENDERSON, CHARLES R.	"	"
HOOPER, J. P.	"	"
HOOPER, WILLIAM B.	"	"
HUGHES, JOHN.	"	"
JAMESON, ROBERT C.	"	"

NAME.	RESIDENCE.	YEAR.
Jenkins, Charles K.	Baltimore.	1852
Jenkins, Edw.	"	"
Jenkins, Joseph William.	"	"
Keilholtz, Otis.	"	"
Kennedy, William.	"	"
Keny, John England.	"	"
King, Thomas F. X.	"	"
Lavender, B. A.	"	"
Lemnon, James A.	Virginia.	"
Lemnon, W. S.	Baltimore.	"
Mathews, Charles H.	"	"
McCauley, M.	"	"
McNeal, James.	"	"
McSherry, H. F.	"	"
Moale, Henry.	"	"
Neale, E. Clarence.	"	"
Nicholson, J. A.	"	"
O'Brien, John.	"	"
Puhl, J. Henry.	"	"
Semmes, C. W.	"	"
Sindall, H. S.	"	"
Smith, W. J.	"	"
Silcox, J. Ignatius.	"	"
Tiernan, C. B.	"	"
Thomas, F.	"	"
Vallego, Andronico.	"	"
Verrier, Florentio.	Cuba.	"
Wilson, Augustus.	Baltimore.	"
Wilson, James.	"	"

Faculty of St. Mary's Seminary, 1891.

FACULTY OF ST. MARY'S SEMINARY, 1891-92.

VERY REV. ALPHONSE MAGNIEN, S. S., *Superior*.
REV. PAULINUS F. DISSEZ, S. S.
REV. ADOLPHE A. TANQUEREY, S. S.
REV. MATHURIN S. ROTHUREAU, S. S.
REV. ARSÈNE BOYER, S. S.
REV. EDUARD R. DYER, S. S.
REV. AUGUSTE M. CHÉNEAU, S. S.
REV. EUGENIUS J. FOREST, S. S.
REV. JOSEPH TRACY.
REV. LEO BESNARD, S. S.
REV. HIPPOLYTE PLUCHON, S. S.

FACULTY OF ST. CHARLES' COLLEGE, 1891-92.

Rev. F. L. M. DUMONT, S. S., *President.*
Rev. P. P. DENIS, S. S.
Rev. A. J. B. VUIBERT, S. S.
Rev. H. F. GRIFFIN.
Rev. H. M. CHAPUIS, S. S.
Rev. G. E. VIGER, S. S.
Rev. S. GUILBAUD, S. S.
Rev. A. S. FONTENEAU, S. S.
Rev. C. V. SCHRANTZ, S. S.
Rev. P. F. ROUX, S. S.
Rev. C. J. JUDGE, S. S.
Rev. R. K. WAKEHAM, S. S.
Rev. A. P. BERNARD, S. S.
Rev. J. M. HAUG, S. S.
Rev. J. B. TABB.
Rev. F. X. McKENNY, S. S.
Mr. H. C. POUGET.
Mr. M. W. KELLOGG.

Faculty of St. Charles' College, 1891.

STUDENTS OF ST. MARY'S SEMINARY,
1891-92.

Deacons.

McKeefry, William Anth.
Malone, Henry Vincent.

Sub-Deacons.

Dus, Otto Joseph.
McManus, Miles Joseph.
Rochard, Augustus Michael.
Brady, Daniel Alphonsus.

Acolytes.

Gilmartin, Mich. Sarsfield.
Langlois, John Marie.
Brown, James Thomas.
O'Neill, James David.
Mallon, Joseph Charles.
Tower, James Patrick.
Ramm, Charles Adolph.
Hegarty, Thomas.
Cull, John Aloysius.
Dooley, Patrick.
Toner, Joseph James.
Demurger, Alexis Joseph.
Hauck, Joseph Bernard.
Wills, Henry James.
Hallissey, Joseph Francis.

Cullinane, Eugene.
Kessler, John Augustine.
Campeau, Ernest.
O'Reilly, Edward Alph.
O'Rourke, Michael Francis.
Flood, Edward James.
Kirwan, Francis William.
Graham, John Andrew.
Furman, Albert.
Foley, Martin Francis.
Solon, James Aloysius.
Lynch, Thomas Patrick.

Lectors.

Burke, Thomas Michael.
McNamara, Lawrence John.
Foley, Joseph Andrew.
Mahon, Joseph Thomas.
Fielding, James Francis.
Fanning, William Joseph.
Blake, William James.
Code, John Joseph.

Clerics.

Ahern, Michael Joseph.
Probey, Henry Aloysius.

Fox, Edward Joseph.
O'Reilly, Michael Joseph.
Murray, Thomas John.
Gaynor, John Patrick.
Ryan, Michael Augustine.
Roche, Joseph Thomas.
Degel, Michael Francis.
Esper, Michael George.
Cronan, Philip Andrew.
LaChance, Napoleon John.
Kiernan, William.
Mies, John Siegfried.
Shine, Michael Allen.
Bennett, John Thomas.
Cushion, Richard Bennet.
Fallon, William Boland.
Kramer, Edward Henry.
Lamb, Joseph Francis.
Eaton, William Henry.
McDonough, Wm. Bernard.
Suerth, John Peter.

LAYMEN.

Hannigan, Edward Francis.
Reynolds, Edward Victor.
Whelan, James Louis.
Walsh, Edward Joseph.
O'Laughlin, Denis Francis.
Dunn, William Francis.
Kearney, Wm. Lawrence.
Griffin, John Joseph.
Bustin, Dennis Joseph.
Parker, John Perren.
Murphy, John Charles.
Reinhardt, Joseph Anton.
Cleary, Frank John.
Duffy, John Thomas.
Hannigan, Jerome Bernard.
Conway, David Joseph.
Dorney, Maurice Aloysius.

Granville, John Charles.
McCarville, Joseph Hyginus.
Lietuvnik, Joseph.
Norris, John William.
Russi, William Henry.
Prendergast, James Henry.
Haarth, Frederick Joseph.
Pawlowski, Boleslaus Anth.
Boland, John Francis.
Murphy, James Henry.
Russell, Edward Mark.
Logue, Charles Augustine.
Kennedy, Cornelius Joseph.
Dooling, Andrew Robert.
O'Brien, Edward Eustace.
Whelan, Miles James.
Rivard, James Richard.
Esper, Peter Henry.
Halloran, Florence Joseph.
Sinnott, George Thomas.
Brady, Hubert Eugene.
Reid, George Joseph.
McMahon, Charles.
Szedvidis, Michael.
Harrigan, Daniel Joseph.
O'Reilly, Bernard Thomas.
Caraher, Francis.
Brisset, Clement Marie.
Armor, James Benner.
Cannon, John Henry.
Dolan, Thomas Stanislaus.
O'Reilly, Bernard Xavier.
Scully, William Vincent.
Carmody, Thomas William.
Guinan, Lawrence Aloysius.
Bidlingmaier, Joseph.
Regan, James Francis.
Kildea, Bernard.
Costigan, Patrick John.
Waldron, Thomas Francis.

PRESENT STUDENTS OF THE SEMINARY.

PHILOSOPHERS.

Bruen, Timothy J.
Foster, Joseph.
Keenan, Denis Clement.
Walsh, Philip Joseph.
Mallin, James Joseph.
Harig, George Louis.
Coughlin, Henry Patrick.
Quinn, James Alexander.
Hagerty, Thomas Joseph.
Goodwin, Eneas Bernard.
Kinsella, William Joseph.
Wunnenberg, Francis A.
Randolph, Bartholomew.
McSweeny, James Laurence.
Smyth, Patrick.
Vogt, William.
Kelly, Edward James.
McCarthy, Daniel William.
Lavelle, Patrick Eugene.
Loughran, John Joseph.
Brownrigg, Thomas Henry.
Murray, John Bernard.
Hughes, Peter James.
Brey, Celestine.
Kelly, Denis Sylvester.
Crowe, John Ambrose.
Heidenreich, Frederick L.
Lochbihler, Theodore.
Herr, Joseph Francis.
Hughes, John Charles.
Reidel, Charles.
Healy, Edward Joseph.
McQuillen, Robert Joseph.
Walsh, Thomas Albert.
Dowling, John William.
Papka, Anthony Stanislaus.
Griffin, Thomas Paul.
O'Dwyer, William Kilian.
Donahue, Martin Richard.
O'Donoghue, Martin John.
Waters, Thomas Edmond.
Fenlon, John Francis.
Thompson, Henry Philip.
Bachand, Louis Seraphin.
McDade, John Vincent.
Kuehnel, Reynold.
Bock, George John.
Krams, Anthony.
Clements, William.
Lacey, Owen.
Lynott, Peter James.
Beauparland, Joseph David.
Brennan, Cornelius John.
Boardman, Henry Francis.
Conway, Joseph John.
Thompson, Thomas William.
McKeon, Eugene Chr.
Beagin, John Bernard.
Leonard, James Henry.
Beavan, Ambrose Otilia.
Noonan, John James.

To the preceding list the following theological students of the class of '92 are to be added:

DEACONS.

Thomas S. Donoghue, at the Catholic University.
Patrick J. Griffin, at the Catholic University.

JOHN F. CONLIN, at the Catholic University.
JOSEPH F. BYRNE, at Santa Clara College, Cal.
JOSEPH P. MCQUAID, at Santa Clara College, Cal.

Sub-Deacons.

JOHN J. BELL, at the Catholic University.
THOMAS J. O'BRIEN, at the Catholic University.
JOSEPH M. GLEASON, at the Catholic University.
JOHN CASSIDY, at St. Ambrose College, Davenport, Ia.

Acolyte.

EDWARD P. DEMPSEY, at the Catholic University.

www.ingramcontent.com/pod-product-compliance
Lightning Source LLC
Chambersburg PA
CBHW021829230426
43669CB00008B/911